Visual Basic 6.0 Tutorials

By Peterson

Table of Contents

Introduction

Visual Basic is a high level programming language developed by Microsoft with the help of Alan Cooper and was first released in May 1991. BASIC stands for Beginners' All-purpose Symbolic Instruction Code. The program codes in Visual Basic resemble the English language. It was one of the first products to offer a graphical programming environment and a paint metaphor for building up user interfaces. The Visual Basic programmers can put in a large amount of code simply by dragging and dropping controls, such as buttons and forms and then defining their look and behavior. This reduces much concern about syntax details.

Though it is not a true object-oriented programming language, Visual Basic has an object-oriented philosophy. It is visual and event-driven programming language and these are the main differences from the old BASIC. In BASIC for example, programming is through a text-based environment and the program is executed in order, but in Visual Basic, programming is done in a graphical environment. In old Basic, one has to write a text-based procedure to design the interface, but Visual Basic you design the interface by dragging the controls, resizing as well as changing their colors, simply like any windows-based application. It is event driven because each object can react to different events such as a mouse click and entering text into a textbox.

Since its introduction in 1990, the Visual Basic approach has become the standard for programming languages. Currently there are visual environments for various programming languages, including C, C++, Pascal, and Java. It is sometimes called a Rapid Application

Development (RAD) system as it enables programmers to quickly develop prototype applications.

Visual Basic is a quite easy programming language to study and it is for anybody who is interested in programming but lack proficient training in software engineering. Learning VB will help kids to improve their logical thinking skills and expand their minds. One can choose to program in VB just for fun and enjoyment or one can build more advanced applications such as educational projects and business-related software.

Getting Started with Visual Basic 6.0

Visual Basic is initiated by using the Programs option > Microsoft Visual Basic 6.0 > Visual Basic 6.0 and click the Visual Basic icon. Upon start up, Visual Basic 6.0 will display the following dialog box as shown in Figure below.

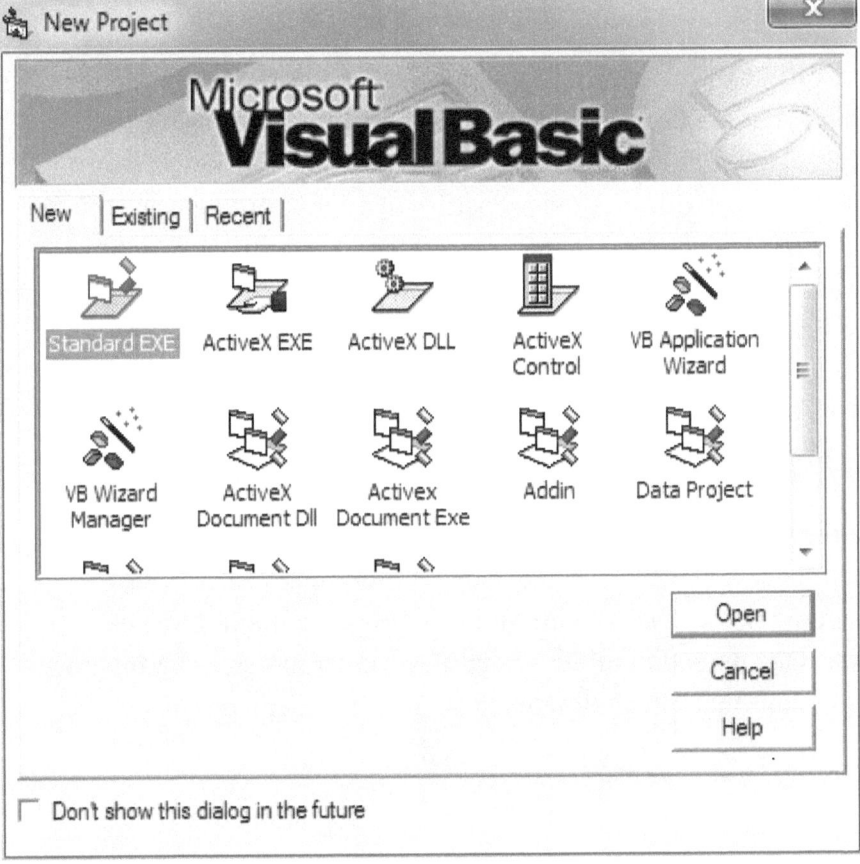

Click on Standard EXE, this means executable program. This will open the VB programming environment as shown below.

The **Visual Basic Environment** consists of a blank form for you to design your application's interface, the **project window** which displays the files that are created in your application, the **properties window** which displays the properties of various controls and objects that are created in your application. It also has a **Toolbox** that consists of all the controls essential for developing a VB Application. The controls include text boxes, command buttons, labels, combo boxes etc

Main Window

On the **Main Window** we find the title bar, menu bar, and toolbar. The title bar shows the project name, the current Visual Basic operating mode, and the current form. From the **menu bar** you control the operation of the Visual Basic environment. The **toolbar** has buttons that offer shortcuts to some of the menu options.

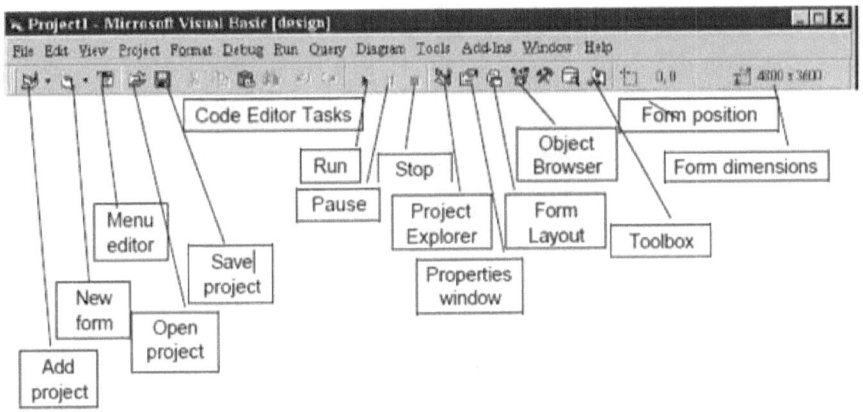

Form Window

The **Form Window** is vital to developing an applications. It is where we design the application.

Toolbox

The **Toolbox** is the selection menu for **controls** used in your application.

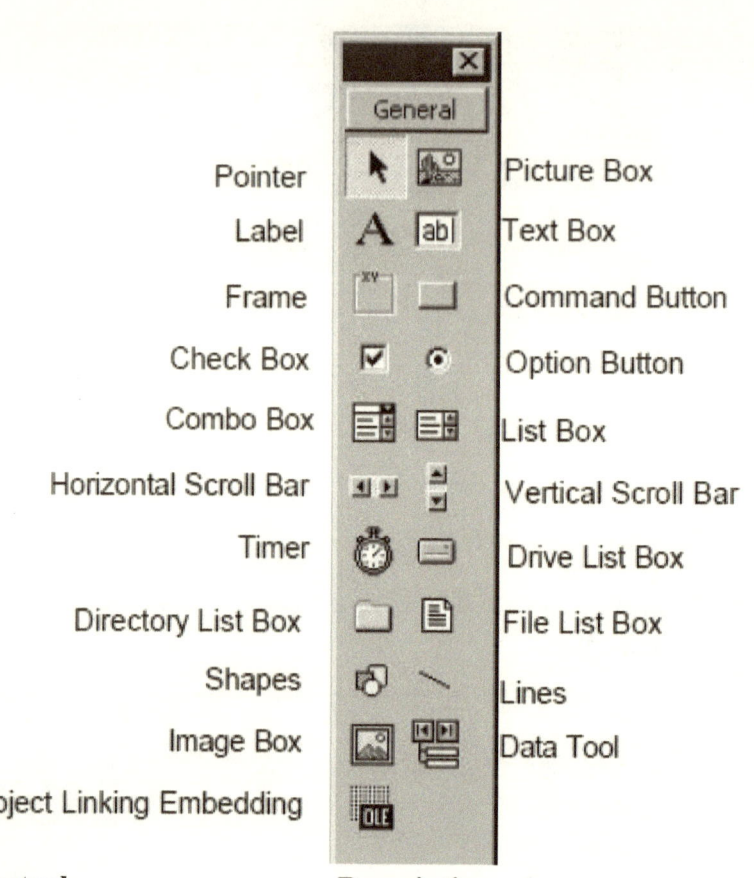

Control	Description

Pointer   Provides a way to move and resize the controls
on the form.

Label   Displays a text that the user cannot modify e.g
First name

TextBox   Used to display message and enter text.

Frame   Serves as a diagram and functional container for
controls.

CommandButton   Used to carry out the specified action when the
user clicks it. It is where we   write most of
the codes

CheckBox   Displays a True/False or Yes/No option. One
can choose **more than one** option

OptionButton	Option Button control which is a part of an option group allows the user to select **only one** option from multiple choices.
ListBox	Displays a list of items from which a user can select one.
ComboBox	This allows the user to select an item from the dropdown List.
HScrollBar and VScrollBar	These controls allow the user to select a value within the specified range of values
Timer	Carries outs the timer events at specified intervals of time
DriveListBox	Displays the available disk drives and allows the user to select one of them.
DirListBox	Let s the user to select the directories and paths, which are displayed.
FileListBox	Shows a set of files from which a user can select the one.
Shape	Used to add shape to a Form e.g a rectangle
Line	Used to draw straight line to the Form
Image	used to display images on the form
Data	Enables one to connect to an existing database and show information from it.
OLE	It is used to link to an object, show and use data from other windows based applications.

The **Properties Window** is located on the right hand of the screen and its used to change the characteristics of elements on the form. Two views are available, that is Alphabetic and Categorized. All these characteristics of an object are called its properties. Both forms and any controls placed on it will have properties.

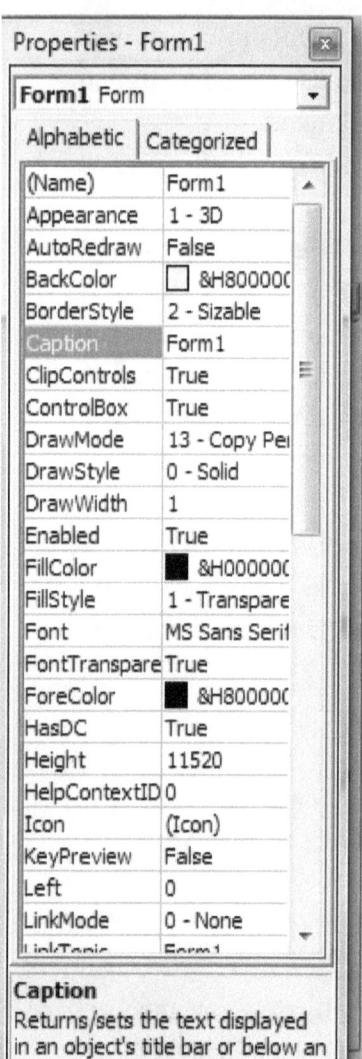

Project Window

The **Project Window** displays a list of all forms and modules making up your application. You can also obtain a view of the Form or Code windows from the Project window. It is possible to add more forms here.

Object naming conversions of controls (prefix)

Name of Control	Prefix
Form	frm
Label	lbl
TextBox	txt
CommandButton	cmd
CheckBox	chk
OptionButton	opt
ComboBox	cbo
ListBox	lst
Timer	tmr
Frame	frm
PictureBox	pic
Image	img
Shape	shp
Line	lin
HScrollBar	hsb
VScrollBar	vsb

Rules to follow when naming elements in VB

- A name must start with a letter.

- May be as much as 255 characters long

- Must not contain a space or an embedded period or type-declaration characters used to specify a data type; these are ! # % $ & @

- Must not be a reserved word

- The dash, although its okey, should be avoided because it may be confused with the minus sign.

The Controls

The Label

The label is a very useful control for Visual Basic. It holds static text. It's used to provide instructions and guides to the users and also to display outputs. **Caption** is one of its most important properties.

NAME

ADMISSION NO.

YEAR OF BIRTH

The Text Box

It is a control that is used to get input from the user and display the output. It can hold string (text) and numeric data **but not** images or pictures.

Allan

CI001

Strings in a text box can be changed to numeric data by with the function **Val(text).** E.g

txtsum=Val(txtfirstno) + val(txtsecondno)

The Command Button

The command button is used to execute commands. The most common event associated with the command button is the Click event. It is where we write most of the codes. The syntax is:

Private Sub Cmdcalculate_Click ()
*Txtvolume = Txtlength * Txtwidth * Txtheight*

End Sub

By clicking on the command button *calculate*, textbox *txtvolume* will give us the volume, i.e the product of the values of textboxes *txtlength, txtwidth and txtheight.*

The Combo Box

The purpose of the Combo Box is also to offer a list of items where the user can click and select the items from the list. The user needs to click on the pull down on the right of the combo box to see the items which are presented in a list. In order to add items to the list, you can also use the **AddItem** method.

For example, if you wish to add a number of items to Combo box 1, you can key in the following statements:

Private Sub Form_Load()
Combo1.Additem "2014"
Combo1.Additem "2015"
Combo1.Additem "2016"
Combo1.Additem "2017"
Combo1.Additem "2018"
Combo1.Additem "2019"

End Sub

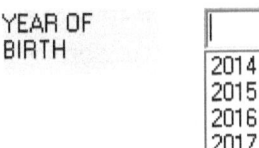

YEAR OF
BIRTH

2014
2015
2016
2017
2018
2019

The Check Box

The Check Box control lets the user select or unselect an option. Its value is set to 1 when the Check Box is checked, and when it is unchecked, the value is set to 0. It gives a user a chance to make more than one choice.

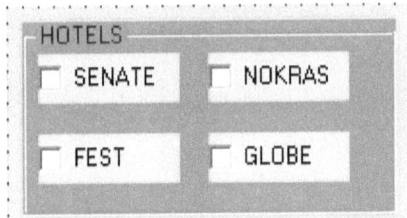

HOTELS

☐ SENATE   ☐ NOKRAS

☐ FEST   ☐ GLOBE

The Option Box

The Option Box control allows the user to select one of the choices. However, two or more option Boxes must work together because as one of the Option Boxes is selected, the other one will be unselected. NB In fact, only one Option Box can be selected at one time. When an option box is selected, its value is set to "True" and its value is set to "False" when it is unselected.

The List Box

The purpose of the List Box is to present a list of items where the user can click and select items from the list. We can use the *AddItem*method in order to add items to the list.

The Picture Box

The Picture Box is one of the controls that used to handle graphics. You can insert a picture during the designing stage by clicking on the picture item in the properties window and select the picture from the desired folder.

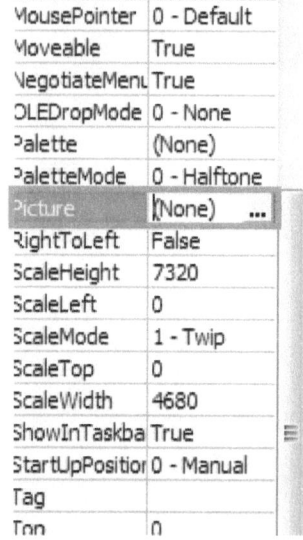

The Image Box

The Image Box also handles images and pictures. It purposes are almost the same as the picture box, though, there is one key difference, that is the image in an Image Box is stretchable, which means it can be resized.

The Drive List Box

The Drive ListBox is used to show a list of drives available in your computer. You will be able to select different drives from your computer when you put this control into the form and run the program.

The Directory List Box

The Directory List Box is used to show the list of directories or folders in a selected drive. You will be able to select different directories from a selected drive in your computer when you place this control into the form and run the program.

The File List Box

The File List Box is used to display the list of files in a selected directory or folder. You will be able to a list of files in a selected directory when you place this control into the form and run the program.

The Properties of the Controls

You have to set certain properties for the control to determine its appearance and how it will work with the program. Set the properties of the controls in the properties window or at runtime.

For example, one can rename the form name, caption, fill color, font etc to any name that you like best. In the properties window, the name property appears at the top part is the object currently. Properties can be set by selecting the items and then changing them by typing or selecting the options available.

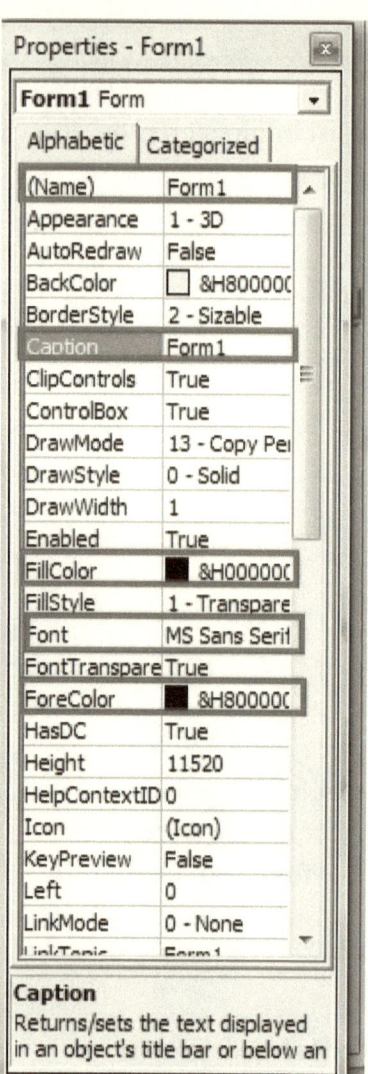

In order to change the caption for example, select Form1 and under the **Name** property change it to your preferred name e.g **frmenrolment** and for **Caption** and change it to **Enrolment**. You can also modify the look of the form by setting it to 3D or flat. You can also alter properties like the **foreground** and **background color**, changing the **font type** and **font size**, **enabling** or **disabling** the **minimize** and **maximize** buttons etc.

Repeat the above procedure to change the properties of other controls like textbox, label, combo box.

Important points about setting up the properties

- Set the Caption Property of a control clearly so that a user knows what to do with that control. For example, Enrolment program, set the captions such as First Name, Surname, Admission No etc

- Use a meaningful name for the Name Property to make it easier for others to write and read the Program and debug without much problem for example frmenrolment, frmcalculator, txtsurname etc . Another method is to use comments in the program whenever necessary.

Data Types

Visual Basic variables are of variant by default. This means they can store numeric, date/time or string data. When a variable is stated, a data type is supplied for it that determines the kind of data they can store. Visual Basic supports other data types. Each data type has limits to the type of information and the minimum and maximum values it can store.

1. Numeric

Byte   Store integer values in the range of 0 - 255

Integer   Store integer values in the range of (-32,768) - (+ 32,767)

Long   Store integer values in the range of (-2,147,483,468) - (+ 2,147,483,468)

Single   Store floating point value in the range of (-3.4x10-38) - (+ 3.4x1038)

Double   Store large floating value which exceeding the single data type value

Currency   store monetary values. It supports 4 digits to the right of decimal point and 15 digits to the left

2. String

Use to store alphanumeric values. A variable length string can store approximately 4 billion characters

3. Date

Use to store date and time values. A variable declared as date type can store both date and time values and it can store date values 01/01/0100 up to 12/31/9999

4. Boolean

Thesse data types hold either a true or false value. These are not stored as numeric values and cannot be used as such. Values are internally stored as -1 (True) and 0 (False) and any non-zero value is considered as true.

5. Variant

Stores any type of data and is the default Visual Basic data type. In Visual Basic if we declare a variable without any data type by default the data type is assigned as default.

Variable Declaration

There are three ways for a variable to be declared:
- Default
- Implicit
- Explicit

If variables are not implicitly or explicitly typed, they are assigned the variant type by **default**. The variant data type is a special type used by VB that can contain numeric, string, or date data.

To **implicitly** type a variable, use the corresponding suffix shown above in the data type table. For example:
Bsal = "This is a string";
This creates a string variable,
But Sal = 300; creates an integer variable.

To **explicitly** type a variable, you must first determine its scope. Four levels of scope are available:
1. Procedure level
2. Procedure level, static
3. Form and module level
4. Global level

Operators in Visual Basic

Arithmetical Operators

Operators	Description	Example	Result
+	Add	15+5	20
-	Substract	10-3	7

24

/	Divide	40/5	8	
\	Integer Division	20\3	6	
*	Multiply	5*7	35	
^	Exponent (power of)	3^3	27	
Mod	Remainder of division	20 Mod 6	2	
&	String concatenation	"Peter"&" "&"Son"	"Peter Son"	

Relational Operators

Operat ors	Description	Example	Result
>	Greater than	30>20	True
<	Less than	35<20	False
>=	Greater than or equal to	40>=20	True
<=	Less than or equal to	20<=30	True
<>	Not Equal to	8<>5	True
=	Equal to	15=25	False

Logical Operators

Operators	Description
OR	Operation will be true if either of the operands is true
AND	Operation will be true only if both the operands are true

Building the Visual Basic Applications

Steps in Building a Visual Basic Application

Launch Microsoft Visual Basic. A default form Form1 will appear to start you're the new project. Double click on Form1 the get the source code window.

Type the text under Private Sub Form_Load()

Private Sub Form_Load()
Form1.Show
Print "Hello. This is Vb 6.0 Program"

End Sub

Note the statement should be between Private Sub Form_Load() and End Sub statement. Print statement displaying the output of the program on the screen.

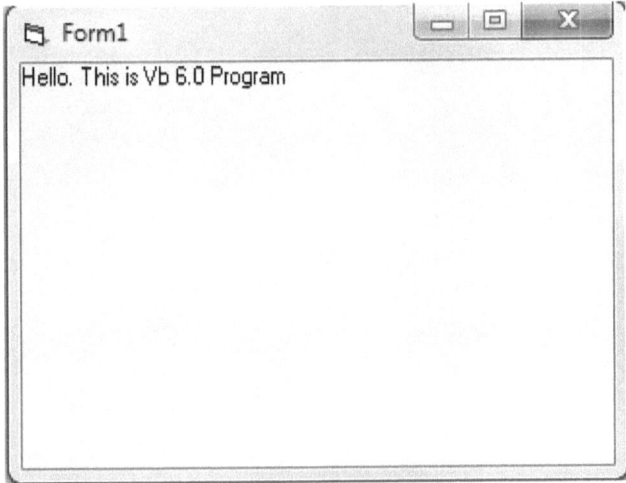

The three basic steps in building a VB application are as follows:
- Design the interface
- Set the properties of the controls
- Write the events' procedures

Example 1. To display a sum of the two numbers

Open a new Standard EXE project and the save the Form as Sum.frm and save the project as calculation.vbp.

In this example, three text boxes are inserted into the form together with a three labels. The two text boxes are used to accept inputs from the user and one to display the sum of the two numbers. Labels will be used to display the contents of text boxes. A command button is programmed to calculate the sum of the two numbers using the plus operator. The program creates a variable, '*sum*', to accept the summation of values from the two text boxes.

Design the Form as per the following specifications table.

Object	Property	Settings
Label	Caption	*First Number*
	Name	*Lblfirstno*

27

Label	Caption	Second Number
	Name	Lblsecondno

Label	Caption	Sum
	Name	Lblsum

Textbox	Text	Empty
	Name	Txtfno

Textbox	Text	Empty
	Name	Txtsno

Textbox	Text	Empty
	Name	Txtsum

Commandbutton	Caption	Calculate
	Name	Cmdcalculate

Double click command button and enter the following code:

```
Private Sub Cmdcalculate_Click()
Txtsum = Val(Txtfno.Text) + Val(Txtsno.Text)

End Sub
```

Run the program and enter first number and Second number and the click command calculate. The program will display the output.

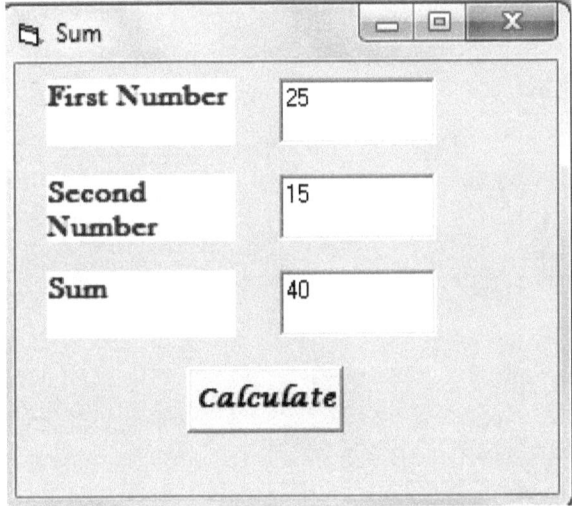

Example 2. A program to calculate the volume of a cuboid

First go to the properties window and change the form caption to Volume and insert four labels and four Text Boxes into the form. Clear textboxes' contents so that you get four empty boxes. Name the text boxes as *Txtlength, Txtwidth, Txtheight* and *Txtvolume*. Lastly, insert three command buttons and change their caption to *Calculate, Delete* and *Close*. Change their names to *CmdCalc, CmdDel* and *CmdClose*.

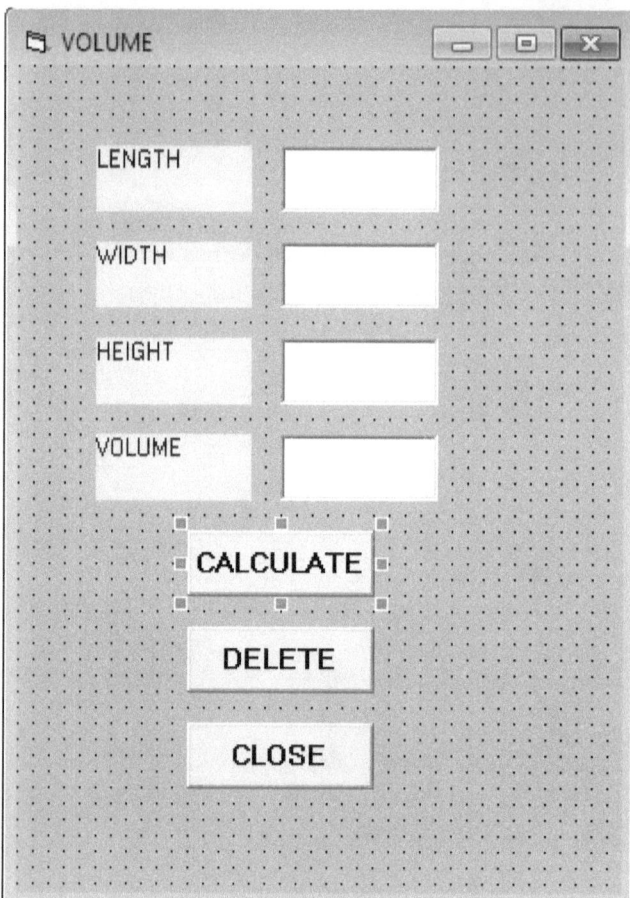

Use command **Delete** to delete the textboxes' contents and command
Close to close the program.
Double click each of the three command button buttons and Enter
the codes as shown in the image below.

```
Private Sub CMDCALC_Click()
TXTVOLUME.Text = TXTLENGTH.Text * TXTWIDTH.Text * TXTHEIGHT.Text

End Sub

Private Sub CMDCLOSE_Click()
Unload Me

End Sub

Private Sub CMDDEL_Click()
TXTLENGTH.Text = ""
TXTWIDTH.Text = ""
TXTHEIGHT.Text = ""
TXTVOLUME.Text = ""

End Sub
```

Now save the project and the form. Run the program, enter your preferred units and click command calculate. This will give the volume of the cuboid. Command delete will the contents and command close will close the program.

Example 3. A simple Student Registration Program

Go to the properties window and change the form caption to *Registration* and insert four labels for *First Name, Second name, County* and *Date of Birth*. Next insert three Text Boxes into the form. Clear textboxes' contents so that you get three empty textboxes. Name the text boxes as *TxtFname, TxtSname* and *TxtCounty*.

Insert a frame and change its caption to Gender. Inside the frame draw two optionbuttons and caption them as *Male* and *female*.

Insert another frame and give it a caption as Courses and draw four checkboxes and give the captions depending on the preferred courses. In the example below I have listed four popular courses i.e Engineering, Teaching, Medical and Accounting.

Next insert a Combobox next to date of birth label as shown below. To give the content to the combobox remember we double click the form and under private sub Form load we insert the code as shown below.

Private Sub Form_Load()

CBODOB.AddItem "1988"
CBODOB.AddItem "1989"
CBODOB.AddItem "1990"
CBODOB.AddItem "1991"
CBODOB.AddItem "1992"
CBODOB.AddItem "1993"
CBODOB.AddItem "1994"
CBODOB.AddItem "1995"
CBODOB.AddItem "1996"
CBODOB.AddItem "1997"
CBODOB.AddItem "1998"
CBODOB.AddItem "1999"
CBODOB.AddItem "2000"
CBODOB.AddItem "2001"

End Sub

Now save the project and the form. Run the program, enter your preferred names and county, choose the gender, on the combobox choose the date of birth and finally check the preferred course. Try to add command close to the program.

Example 4. A Program which can accept three subject, calculate total and average

Go to the properties window and change the form caption to **Results** and insert eight labels for **Student Name, Adm No, Date of Birth, three subjects, Total** and **Average**. Next insert seven Text Boxes into the form. Clear textboxes' contents so that you get seven empty textboxes. Name the text boxes as **Txtname, Txtadm, Txtmaths, Txtart, Txtmusic, Txttotal, and Txtavg.** Insert one combobox between maths and year of birth, clear its contents and give it name as **CboYOB**. Create three command buttons ie. Calculate, delete and close.

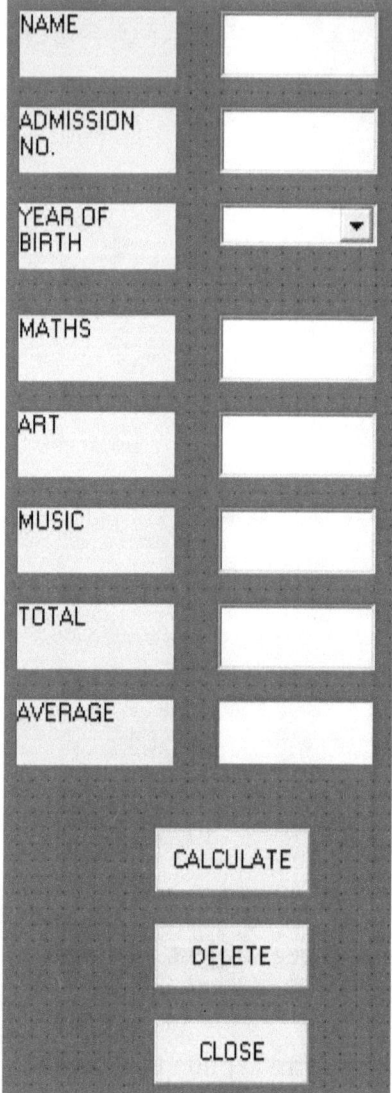

Double click command calculate and enter the code to calculate total and another one to calculate the average.

Txttotal.Text = Val(Txtmaths.Text) + Val(Txtart.Text) + Val(Txtmusic.Text)

Txtavg.Text =Val(Txttotal.Text / 3)

Note that average is divided by three because the number of the subjects.
Double command Delete and enter the code below to delete the text on the textboxes and on the combobox.

Txtname.text= ""
Txtadm.text= ""
Cboyob.text= ""
Txtmaths.Text= ""
Txtart.Text= ""
Txtmusic.Text= ""
Txttotal.Text = ""
Txtavg.Text = ""

Run the program and enter the name, admin no, choose the year of birth and enter the marks for the three subjects. Click command calculate and note the total marks and the average.

Loops (Repetition Structures) in Visual Basic 6

A loop is a repetition structure that allows one to repeat an action until given condition is met.

Types of loops

   i.   For.......Next
   ii.   Do........Loop
   iii.   While.....Wend

For next

The **For...Next** Loop is popular way to make loops in Visual Basic. It uses a counter variable. The following loop counts the numbers from 1 to 50:

Private sub cmdcalculate_Click()

```
Dim c,n As Integer
n=0
For c = 1 To 50
n=n+1
Print n
Next
End sub
```

In the above example we use the two variables i.e c and n to represent counter and number variables. Then we initialize the value of number to zero. The program adds one to each time to loop from one to last one until the counter reaches 50.

To generate a different format for example 10,20,30,40 up to a 100th term, use the example below:

```
Private sub cmdcalculate_Click()

Dim c, n As Integer
n=0
For c = 1 To 100
n=n+10
Print n
Next
End sub
```

Exit For

Exit for is used when a user might want to get out of the loop before the whole process is executed. It is place within the loop. It is used with the If……. Then statement. For example, let's assume we want to exit the above loop when the number is greater than or equal to 100.

```
Private sub cmdcalculate_Click()

Dim c, n As Integer
n=0
For c = 1 To 100
n=n+10
If n>=100 Then
Exit For
End If
Print n
Next
End sub
```

The loop exits when the number is greater than or equal to 100.

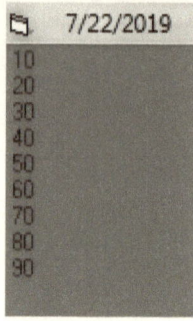

Do Loop

    i.   Do Until ….Loop

    ii.   Do…Loop While

Do Until…..Loop Statement

Statements in the body of a **Do Until...Loop** are executed repeatedly as long as the loop-continuation test evaluates to False.

The coding is typed within the click event of the command button.

Private sub Cmdcalc_Click()

Dim n As Integer
n=0
Do Until n >= 100
n = n + 5
Print n
Loop

End sub

Numbers with this format 5, 10, 15, 20 will be displayed on the form as soon as you click on the command button. The loop will stop when the number reaches 100. This is because of the condition.

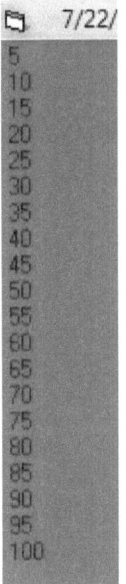

Do...Loop While

The **Do...Loop While** statement first executes the statements and then tests the condition. i.e after each execution. Example:

```
Dim n As integer
n = 0
Do
n = n + 10
Loop While number < 200
```

The programs executes the statements between Do and Loop While structure in any case. Then it determines whether the counter is less than 200. If so, the program again executes the statements between Do and Loop While else exits the Loop. Exit Do is used to exit the Do Loop before the whole process is executed. It is placed within the loop like case for For..Loop.

While.....Wend

A **While...Wend** statement behaves like the **Do While...Loop**. The following **While...Wend** counts from 10 to 100

```
Dim n As Integer
n = 0
While n <=100
n = n + 10
Print n
Wend
```

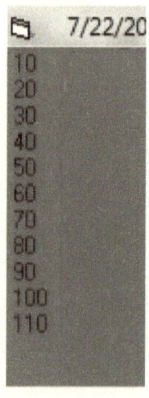

Control Structures in Visual Basic 6.0

Control Statements are used to control the flow of program's execution. Visual Basic supports control structures such as if... Then, if...Then ...Else, Select...Case, and Loop structures such as Do While...Loop, While...Wend, For...Next etc method.

If...Then selection structure

The **If...Then** selection structure performs an indicated action only when the condition is **True**, otherwise the action is ignored. i.e it tests whether a condition and if it is true, the statement is taken, if it is false the statement is ignored.

Syntax of the **If...Then** selection:

If <condition> Then
statement
End If

Example

Write a program to test if a person is eligible to vote. Those below 18 years are illegible to vote.

```
Private Sub Cmdcalc_Click()
Dim a As Integer
a = InputBox("Enter Age")
If a > 18 Then
MsgBox ("Eligible to vote!!!")
End If

End Sub
```

Note that after running the program, the program prompts you to enter the age.

Enter any number greater than 18 and click okey.

The condition is true, therefore the statement between If and End if is executed.

Lastly, enter a number which is less than 18 and click okey.

Note that the statement is ignored. The **If...Then** selection structure test a condition and if its false its ignored. Therefore it can be used if there is more than one condition.

The If...Then...Else selection structure

The **If...Then...Else** selection structure allows the programmer to specify that a different action is to be performed If the condition is False.

Syntax of the If...Then...Else selection

If <condition > Then
Statements
Else
statements
End If

Example 1

Lets use the above program but add an **Else**

```
Private Sub Cmdcalc_Click()
Dim a As Integer
a = InputBox("Enter Age")
If a > 18 Then
MsgBox ("Eligible to vote!!!")
Else
MsgBox ("Too Young to vote!!!")
End If

End Sub
```

After running the program, the program prompts you to enter the age.

Enter any number greater than 18 and click Ok

The condition is true, there the statement is taken

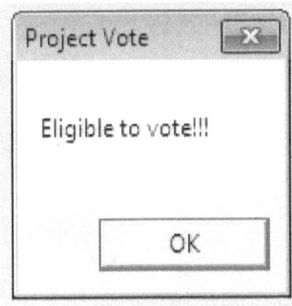

Next enter a number which is less than 18 and click Ok.

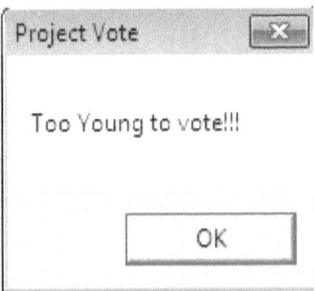

The condition is false and there the statement under the Else is executed. So the **If...Then...Else** selection structure can be used when we have a true and a false condition.

Example 2

A program to award a grade.

```
Private Sub cmdcalculate_Click ()
 If average>50 Then
txtGrade.Text = "Pass"
Else
txtGrade.Text = "Fail"
End If
End Sub
```

If the condition is true the grade will **Pass** and it is False, the grade will be **Fail**.

The **If...Then...Else** selection structure cannot be used to test multiple cases, that is if we have more than two conditions.

Nested If...Then...Else selection structure

Nested If...Then...Else selection structures test for multiple cases. It tests a condition under the **IF** statement, if it is found to be true it is executed. If it is found to be false, it tests the condition in the **ELSE IF**, if it is true it is executed, if it is false it tests the condition under the next **ELSE IF** conditions until the condition is true. **Nested If...Then...Else** can also be used together with logical operators **AND** or **OR**.

Format

If < condition a > Then
statements
ElseIf < condition b > Then
statements
ElseIf < condition c > Then
statements
Else
Statements
End If

An Example, we use the previous program to calculate total and average, add a label and a text box. A label named Grade and a textbox txtgrade.

Grading table

Marks	Grade
80-100	A
60-79	B
50-59	C

| 30-49 | D |
| < 30 | Fail |

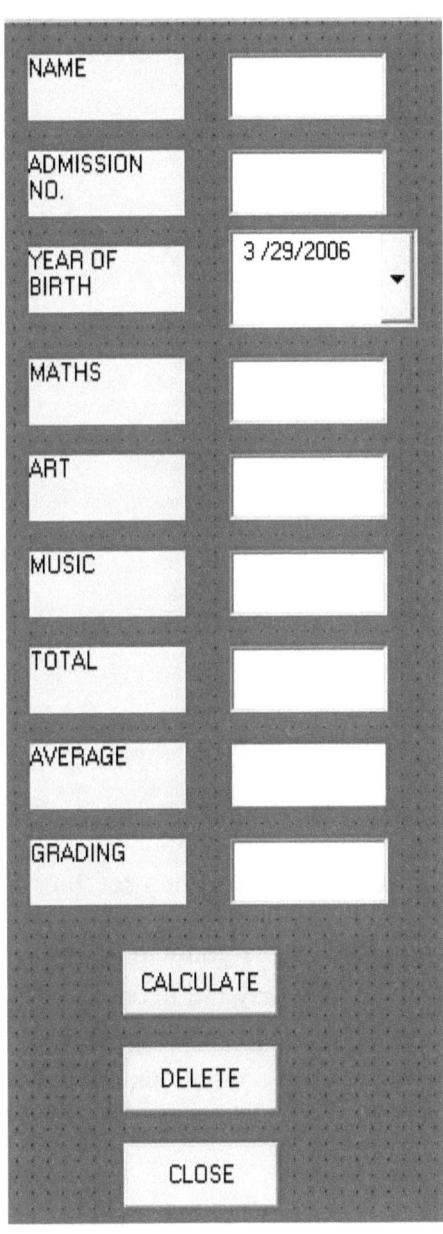

Double click command calculate and enter the code to calculate total and another one to calculate the average.

Private Sub CmdCalc_Click()

Txttotal.Text = Val(Txtmaths.Text) + Val(Txtart.Text) + Val(Txtmusic.Text)

Txtavg.Text =Val(Txttotal.Text / 3)

If Txtavg.Text >= 80 And Txtavg.Text <= 100 Then
Txtgr.text = "A"
ElseIf Txtavg.Text >= 60 And Txtavg.Text <= 79 Then
Txtgr.text = "B"
ElseIf Txtavg.Text >= 50 And Txtavg.Text <= 59 Then
Txtgr.text = "C"
ElseIf Txtavg.Text >= 30 And Txtavg.Text <= 49 Then
Txtgr.text = "D"
Else
Txtgr.text = "Fail"
End If

End Sub

Run the program, enter the details and the grade displayed.

Using Nested If...Then...Else to validate data entered in a textbox

When you give your program to inexperienced users you will realize that some of them will enter invalid data or they may fail to enter required data. This may make your program come to an abrupt end with a run-time error or it may deliver false results. What you really need is a method to trap invalid values.

Example 1

Let's use the previous program to test whether the user has entered the required data and whether the data is valid.

Double click command calculate

Private Sub cmdcalc_Click()

If Txtname.text = "" Then

MsgBox " Name is Required"

Txtname.SetFocus

ElseIf IsNumeric(Txtname.Text) Then

MsgBox "Numbers are not allowed in this textbox"

Txtname = ""

Txtname.SetFocus

End If

If Txtadm.text = "" Then

MsgBox "Please enter your Admission number"

Txtadm.SetFocus

ElseIf Not IsNumeric(Txtadm.text) Then

MsgBox "Only numbers are allowed"

Txtadm.text = ""

Txtadm.SetFocus

End If

If Txtmaths.text = "" Then

MsgBox "Enter your Maths results"

TxtMaths.SetFocus

```
ElseIf Not IsNumeric(Txtmaths.text) Then

MsgBox "Only numbers are allowed"

Txtmaths.text = ""

TxtMaths.SetFocus

End If

If TxArt.text = "" Then

MsgBox "Enter your Art results"

TxtArt.SetFocus

ElseIf Not IsNumeric(TxArt.text) Then

MsgBox "Only numbers are allowed"

TxArt.text = ""

TxArt.SetFocus

End If

If TxMusic.text = "" Then

MsgBox "Enter your Music results"

TxMusic.SetFocus

ElseIf Not IsNumeric(TxMusic.Text) Then

'MsgBox "Only numbers are allowed"

TxMusic.Text = ""

TxMusic.SetFocus

End If
```

```
Txttotal.Text = Val(Txtmaths.Text) + Val(Txtart.Text) +
Val(Txtmusic.Text)

Txtavg.Text =Val(Txttotal.Text / 3)

If Txtavg.Text >= 80 And Txtavg.Text <= 100 Then
Txtgr.text = "A"
ElseIf Txtavg.Text >= 60 And Txtavg.Text <= 79 Then
Txtgr.text = "B"
ElseIf Txtavg.Text >= 50 And Txtavg.Text <= 59 Then
Txtgr.text = "C"
ElseIf Txtavg.Text >= 30 And Txtavg.Text <= 49 Then
Txtgr.text = "D"
Else
Txtgr.text = "Fail"
End If
```

End Sub

The above code will check whether the textbox is null (empty), it will give a message that particular data is required. It will check for numeric data (numbers) using *Not IsNumeric* statement and for letters using *IsNumeric* statement. The invalid data will be deleted by for example *TxMusic.Text* = ""code and cursor will be directed on that particular textbox using for example *TxMusic.SetFocus* code.

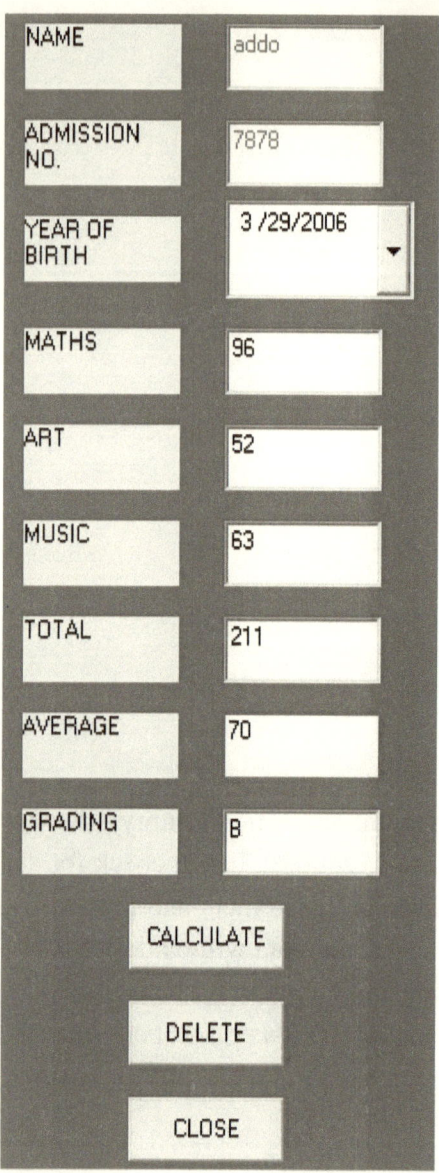

NAME	addo
ADMISSION NO.	7878
YEAR OF BIRTH	3 /29/2006 ▼
MATHS	96
ART	52
MUSIC	63
TOTAL	211
AVERAGE	70
GRADING	B

CALCULATE

DELETE

CLOSE

Example 3 A simple Payroll

Create a simple payroll with the following GUI

Payroll

EMPLOYEE NAME	_____
EMPLOYEE No.	_____
DEPARTMENT	_____ ▼
MARITAL STATUS	_____ ▼
BASIC SALARY	_____
HOUSE ALLOWANCE	_____
MEDICAL ALLOWANCE	_____
GROSS SALARY	_____
SOCIAL CONTRIBUTION	_____
INSURANCE	_____
NET SALARY	_____

[CALCULATE]

[DELETE]

[CLOSE]

Let's start coding the two textboxes, **CBOD** for combobox department and **CBOMS** for combox marital status.

```
Private Sub Form_Load()
''To add Items in a combobox
CBOD.AddItem "Computer"
CBOD.AddItem "Sales"
CBOD.AddItem "Purchases"
CBOD.AddItem "Accounts"
CBOMS.AddItem "Single"
CBOMS.AddItem "Married"

End Sub
```

A code to delete the textboxes and comboboxes

```
Private Sub CMDDEL_Click()
''To delete textboxes's and Comboboxes's contents
TXTE.Text = ""
TXTEN.Text = ""
CBOD.Text = ""
CBOMS.Text = ""
TXTBS.Text = ""
TXTH.Text = ""
TXTM.Text = ""
TXTGS.Text = ""
TXTSOCIAL.Text = ""
TXTINSURE.Text = ""
TXTNS.Text = ""
End Sub
```

The most important Command is command calculate which uses the **Nested If...Then...Else** to prevent invalid data to be entered in the textboxes, empty textboxes and also to calculate basic pay and house allowance.

```
Private Sub cmdcalc_Click()
If TXTE.Text = "" Then
MsgBox "Please enter your Name"
ElseIf IsNumeric(TXTE.Text) Then
MsgBox "Numbers are not allowed in this textbox"
TXTE.Text = ""
TXTE.SetFocus
ElseIf TXTEN = "" Then
MsgBox "Please enter your  employee no."
ElseIf Not IsNumeric(TXTEN.Text) Then
MsgBox "Only numbers are allowed in this textbox"
TXTEN.Text = ""
TXTEN.SetFocus
ElseIf CBOD.Text = "" Then
MsgBox "Please choose your Department"
ElseIf CBOMS.Text = "" Then
MsgBox "Please choose Marital status"

End If
''To calculate Basic Salary
If CBOD.Text = "Computer" Then
TXTBS.Text = 600
ElseIf CBOD.Text = "Sales" Then
TXTBS = 500
ElseIf CBOD.Text = "Purchases" Then
TXTBS.Text = 550
ElseIf CBOD.Text = "Accounts" Then
TXTBS.Text = 525
End If
''To calculate House Allowance
If CBOD.Text = "Computer" Then
txth.Text = 2.5 / 100 * TXTBS.Text
ElseIf CBOD.Text = "Sales" Then
txth.Text = 1.7 / 100 * TXTBS.Text
ElseIf CBOD = "Purchases" Then
txth.Text = 3 / 100 * TXTBS.Text
ElseIf CBOD.Text = "Accounts" Then
txth.Text = 3.2 / 100 * TXTBS.Text
End If
''To calculate Medical Allowance
TXTM.Text = 2 / 100 * Val(TXTBS.Text)
TXTGS.Text = Val(TXTBS.Text) + (Val(txth.Text) + Val(TXTM.Text))
''To calculate Insurance
If CBOMS.Text = "Single" Then
TXTINSURE.Text = 15
ElseIf CBOMS.Text = "Married" Then
TXTINSURE.Text = 20
End If

If TXTBS.Text <= 550 Then
TXTSOCIAL.Text = 1.5 / 100 * Val(TXTGS.Text)
ElseIf TXTBS.Text > 550 Then
TXTSOCIAL.Text = 2.5 / 100 * Val(TXTGS.Text)
```

55

```
End If
TXTNS.Text = Val(TXTGS.Text) - (Val(TXTSOCIAL.Text) + Val(TXTINSURE.Text))

End Sub
```

Example 3 A simple calculator

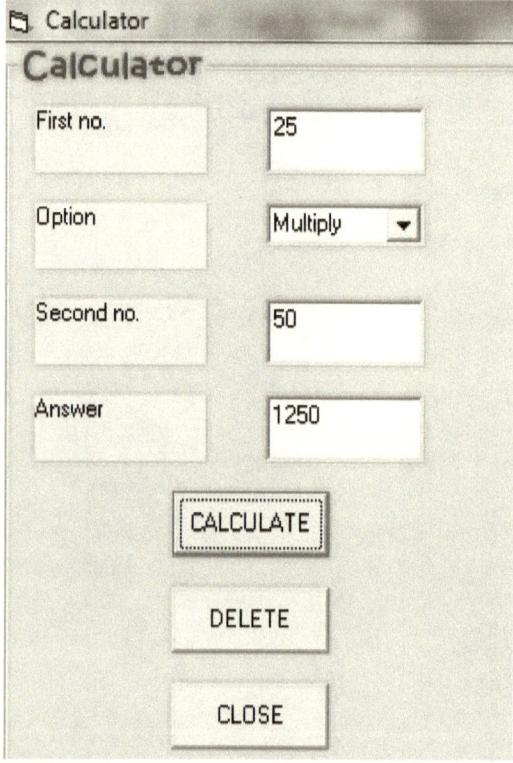

Code

```
Private Sub cmdcalc_Click()
If TXTFirstNo.Text = "" Then
MsgBox "Please enter first number"
ElseIf Not IsNumeric(TXTFirstNo.Text) Then
MsgBox "Only numbers are allowed"
TXTFirstNo.Text = ""
TXTFirstNo.SetFocus
ElseIf TXTSecondNo.Text = "" Then
MsgBox "Please enter second number"
ElseIf Not IsNumeric(TXTSecondNo.Text) Then
MsgBox "Only numbers are allowed"
TXTSecondNo.Text = ""
TXTSecondNo.SetFocus
ElseIf cboOperation.Text = "" Then
MsgBox "Choose an option to calculate"
ElseIf cboOperation.Text = "Multiply" Then
Txtanswer.Text  = Val(TXTFirstNo.Text) * Val(TXTSecondNo.Text)
ElseIf cboOperation.Text = "Divide" Then
Txtanswer.Text = Val(TXTFirstNo.Text) / Val(TXTSecondNo.Text)
ElseIf cboOperation.Text = "Add" Then
Txtanswer.Text = Val(TXTFirstNo.Text) + Val(TXTSecondNo.Text)
ElseIf cboOperation.Text = "Subtract" Then
Txtanswer.Text = Val(TXTFirstNo.Text) - Val(TXTSecondNo.Text)
End If

End Sub
```

Output

In case you click Command calculate without entering the first number, the following error will be displayed.

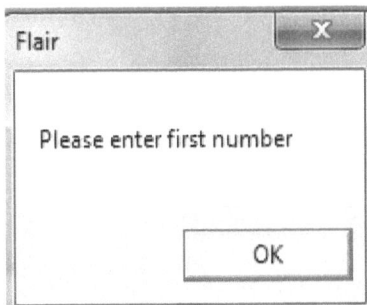

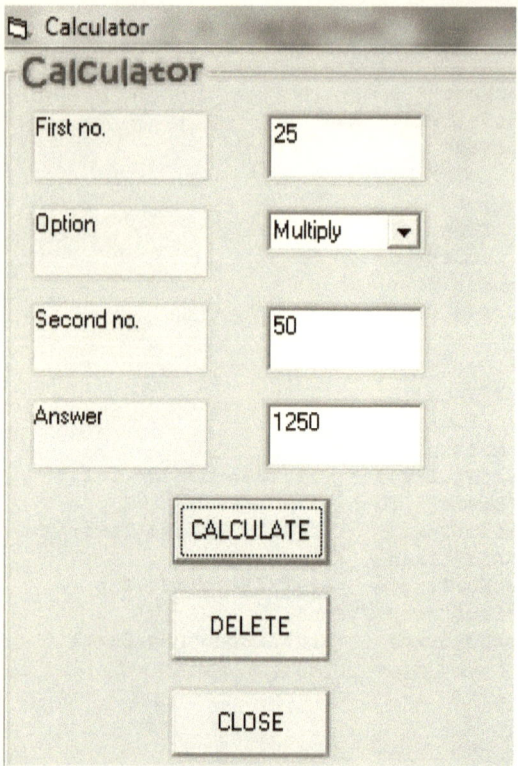

Exercise

Code Commands Delete and close correctly

Select case

In the previous lesson, we have learned how to control the program flow using If...Then...ElseIf control structure. In this lesson, you shall examine another way to control the program flow, that is, the Select Case control structure. The Select Case control structure is slightly different from the If....ElseIf control structure .The difference is that the Select Case control structure can handle conditions with multiple outcomes in an easier manner than the If...Then...ElseIf control structure. The syntax of the Select Case control structure is shown below.

Format

Select Case expression

> *Case value1*
>
>> *Block of one or more VB statements*
>>
>> *Case value2*
>>
>> *Block of one or more VB Statements*
>>
>> *Case Else*
>>
>> *Block of one or more VB Statements*

End Select

Example

```
Private Sub Cmdcalc_Click( )
```
grade=txtgrade.Text
Select Case grade

Case is = "A"
Txtcoment.text="Distinction"
Case is = "B"
Txtcoment.text ="Credit"
Case is = "C"
Txtcoment.text ="Pass"
Case is = "D"
Txtcoment.text ="Fail"
End Select
```
End Sub
```

An example

A school enrolment program using **Select Case** with the following graphical user Interface. Fee is paid depending on the class, therefore branching is required. Fee payable is total of Tuition fee, medical fee, boarding fee, activity fee and uniform fee. Remember to enter the fee payable before clicking command calculate.

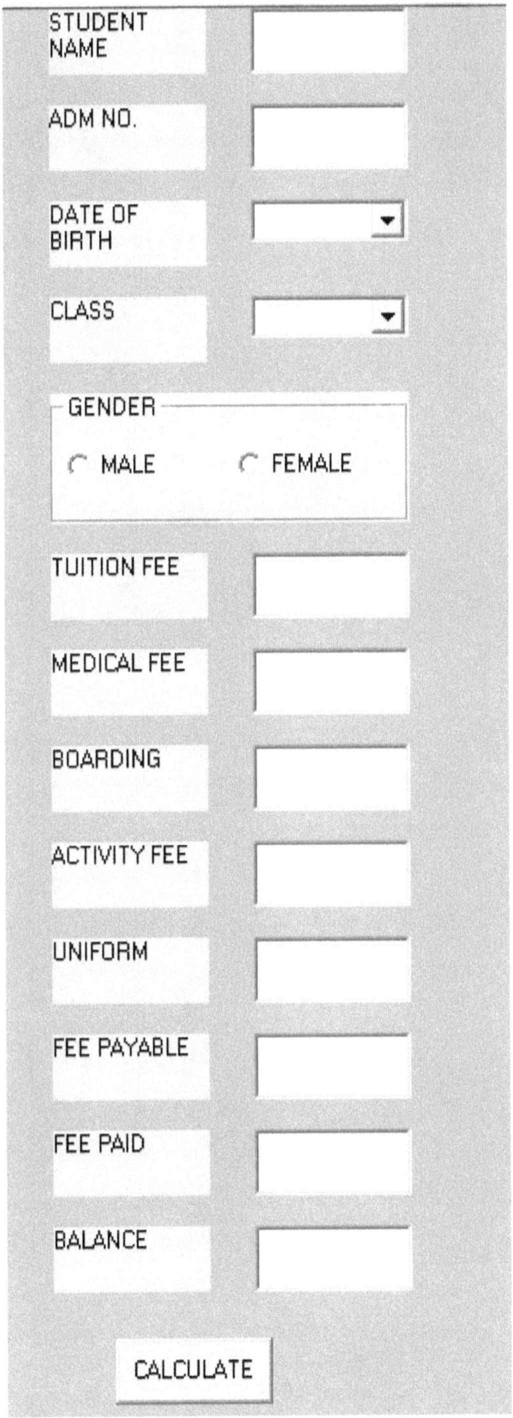

STUDENT NAME	
ADM NO.	
DATE OF BIRTH	▼
CLASS	▼

GENDER

◯ MALE   ◯ FEMALE

TUITION FEE	
MEDICAL FEE	
BOARDING	
ACTIVITY FEE	
UNIFORM	
FEE PAYABLE	
FEE PAID	
BALANCE	

CALCULATE

To add information to the two combo boxes

Private Sub Form_Load()

```
Cbodob.AddItem "1990"
Cbodob.AddItem "1991"
Cbodob.AddItem "1992"
Cbodob.AddItem "1993"
Cbodob.AddItem "1994"
Cbodob.AddItem "1995"
Cbodob.AddItem "1996"
Cbodob.AddItem "1997"
Cbodob.AddItem "1998"
Cbodob.AddItem "1999"
Cboclass.AddItem "4"
Cboclass.AddItem "5"
Cboclass.AddItem "6"
Cboclass.AddItem "7"
Cboclass.AddItem "8"
```

End Sub
Private Sub CmdCalc_Click()

```
Select Case Txtfeepaid
Case Is = ""
MsgBox "Enter the Fees paid"
End Select
Select Case Cboclass
Case Is = "4"
Txtutionfee.Text = 8500
Case Is = "5"
Txtutionfee.Text = 8900
Case Is = "6"
Txtutionfee.Text = 9350
Case Is = "7"
```

```
Txtutionfee.Text = 9550
Case Is = "8"
Txtutionfee.Text = 9700
End Select
Select Case Cboclass
Case Is = "4"
Txtmedicalfee.Text = 350
Case Is = "5"
Txtmedicalfee.Text = 400
Case Is = "6"
Txtmedicalfee.Text = 450
Case Is = "7"
Txtmedicalfee.Text = 500
Case Is = "8"
Txtmedicalfee.Text = 550
End Select
Select Case Cboclass
Case Is = "4"
Txtboardingfee.Text = 4000
Case Is = "5"
Txtboardingfee.Text = 4150
Case Is = "6"
Txtboardingfee.Text = 4250
Case Is = "7"
Txtboardingfee.Text = 4370
Case Is = "8"
Txtboardingfee.Text = 4400
End Select
Select Case Cboclass
Case Is = "4"
Txtactivityfee.Text = 150
Case Is = "5"
Txtactivityfee.Text = 200
Case Is = "6"
```

```
Txtactivityfee.Text = 250
Case Is = "7"
Txtactivityfee.Text = 300
Case Is = "8"
Txtactivityfee.Text = 350
End Select
Select Case Optmale
Case Is = True
Txtuniformfee.Text = 1500
End Select
Select Case Optfemale
Case Is = True
Txtuniformfee.Text = 2000
End Select
Txtfeepayable.Text = Val(Txtutionfee.Text) +
Val(Txtmedicalfee.Text) + Val(Txtboardingfee.Text) +
Val(Txtactivityfee.Text) + Val(Txtuniformfee.Text)
Txtbalance.Text = Val(Txtfeepayable.Text) - Val(Txtfeepaid.Text)

End Sub
```

Exercise

Add Command Delete and Command Close and code them correctly

Message Box Functions

The aim of **MsgBox** function is to create a pop-up message box and prompt the user to click on a command button before continuing.

Format

*Msg=MsgBox(**Prompt, Style Value, Title**)*
The first argument, **Prompt**, will display the message in the message box. The **Style Value** will determine what type of command button to appear on the message box as illustrated in the table below. The **Title** argument will display the title of the message board.

Style Value	Named Constant	Buttons Displayed
0	vbOkOnly	Ok button
1	vbOkCancel	Ok and Cancel buttons
2	vbAbortRetryIgnore	Abort, Retry and Ignore buttons.
3	vbYesNoCancel	Yes, No and Cancel buttons
4	vbYesNo	Yes and No buttons
5	vbRetryCancel	Retry and Cancel buttons

For example:

We can use a message box and a condition to close instead of just unload me, that is before closing the user gets a prompt to confirm whether to close or not. It is more professional to use a message to close because one can click some commands by mistake.
In the above format *Msg* is a variable above holds values that are returned by the MsgBox ( ) function. The values are decided by the type of buttons being clicked by the users. It has to be declared as Integer data type.

Let us change the code of the command close we used to close. Let us look at the normal command code.

```
Private Sub CMDCLOSE_Click()
Unload Me
End Sub
```

Type the variable for example C as Integer. Assign variable as **MsgBox,** give the prompt for example *"Are you sure you want to close"*, **Style value choose** *"vbYesNo"*.

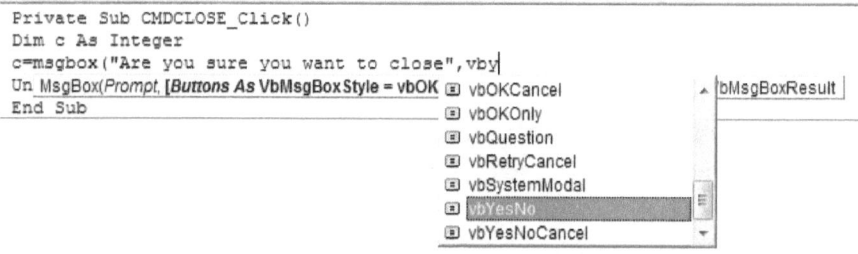

Give **title** as "Close".

```
Private Sub CMDCLOSE_Click()
Dim c As Integer
c=msgbox("Are you sure you want to close",vbYesNo,"Close")
```

Output

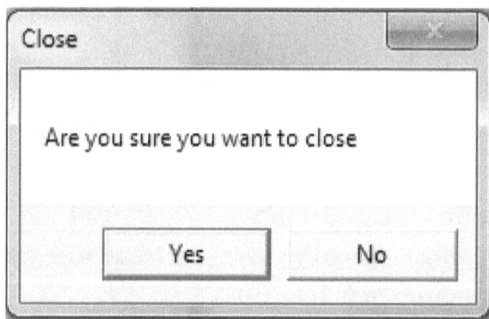

Remember the *if..then* statement. By clicking **Yes** the program will close, but if you click **NO** it will not.

Exercise

Create a close command and include a *vbYesNoCancel* Style valueand a *Confirm*Title.

Working with files

Everything we have covered so far is unfinished. We have created a few programs e.g Volume, Payroll, enrolment, and they are working well but, we can't save the information which we entered, that is we cannot find the data when the program ends. There are various ways to store information for future utilization. The most admired and powerful method is to create a **database**.

Another more accessible method is to create a **data file**. We want to learn how to create and save files by writing them into a storage device and then get it back the data by reading the contents of these files.

Defining new terms

- **A file** is a collection of data on a given subject, stored on a storage medium, e.g a flash disk, Hard disk drive, CD.

- **Record**: one logical section of a file that holds a related set of data. For example if the file contains employee information, a record would hold the information on one employee: *Firstname, Surname, address, employee ID No*, etc. If there are 30 employees, the file contains 30 records.

- **Field**: part of a record that defines a specific information. For example in the employee record, Firstname, Surname, address, employee ID No, are fields. The field is the lowest element in the file. The field is the comparable to a variable. It is called a variable when it is used to store data in **memory** and a field when it stores in a **file**.
- **I/O**: stands for Input/Output. Every time you work with a file you have to have ways of reading data from the file

called **Input** and ways of writing data to the file called **Output**.

Types of files
There are basically three types of files you can work with:

- **Sequential file**: this is where all the information is written in order, that is from the **beginning** to the **end**. To access any record, you have to read all the records stored before that particular record. One can't leap directly to a specific record. It is useful when there is a small amount of data to store. It can also be of use when there is a huge amount of data to be stored, provided the data has to be processed at one time, e.g: a company's report at the end of a trading period.

- **Random file**: this is where all records are available separately. One can jump to any record. This is useful when there is a huge quantity of data to store and it has to be accessible quickly.

- **Binary file**: this is a unique form of the random file. Data is stored at the byte level and you can read and write individual bytes to the file. This makes the file access quick and efficient.

Opening and closing files
The first command to use in a program that needs to work with files is the **Open** command. This assigns the file to a numbered file handle, also called a channel, or sometimes a buffer.

Access Mode
For Mode in the Open statement specify how the file will be used. other modes:

- **Input**: open for sequential input; the file will be read sequentially starting at the beginning.

- **Output**: open for sequential output; records will be written sequentially starting at the beginning and if the file does not exist, it is created. If it does exist, it is overwritten.

- **Random**: open for random read and write; any particular record can be accessed.

- **Append**: sequential output to the end of an existing file. If the file does not exist it is created. This mode does not **overwrite** the file.

- **Binary**: open for binary read and write; access is at byte level.

NB
- For Random is used by default if access mode is not specified in the Open statement
- You need to **Close** all the files that have been opened Once processing is finished
- You can close any number of files with one Close statement. E.g. Close #1, #2, #3

Creating a File

To create a file, use the following statement:

Open "fileName" For Output As #fileNumber

A file name and a file number are used for identification and for the file name, remember also to give the path where the file will saved. For example:

Open "C:\My Documents\Test.txt" For Output As #1

This will create a text file by the name of Test.txt in My Document folder in drive C. The created file number is 1.

Open "D:\Documents\Test.html" For Output As # 2

This will create a text file by the name of Test2.txt in Document folder in drive D. The created file number is 2.

A sample program

```
Private Sub CmdOk_Click()
Dim SName,Country As String,Adm as Integer
Open "C:\My Documents\Test.txt" For Output As #1
SName = InputBox("Enter the student Name")
Print #1, SName
Country = InputBox("Enter the student Country of
origin")
Print #1, Country
Adm = InputBox("Enter the student Admission Number")
Print #1, Adm
Close #1
End Sub
```

Run the program, enter the student name, country and admission number. Lastly check local disk D, find the folder named my documents and open it.

NB

There is a text file named *Test.*

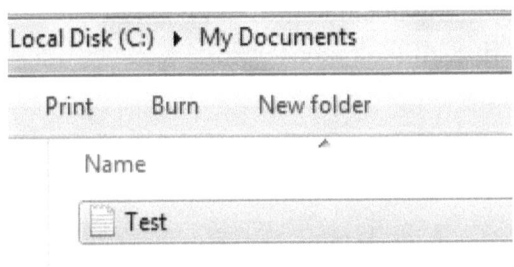

Open the file Test and you will find the student's data.

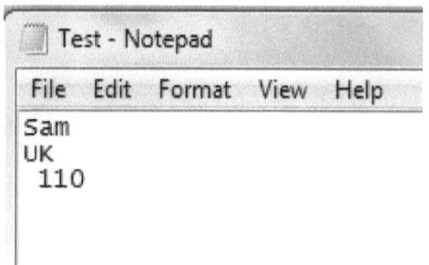

Continue running the program and note that after entering another student's data, this will overwrite the existing record.

We use **Append For** to avoid overwriting the existing record.

```
Private Sub CmdOk_Click()
Dim SName,Country As String,Adm as Integer
Open "C:\My Documents\Test.txt" For Append As #1
SName = InputBox("Enter the student Name")
Print #1, SName
Country = InputBox("Enter the student Country of
origin")
Print #1, Country
Adm = InputBox("Enter the student Admission Number")
Print #1, Adm
Close #1
End Sub
```

Run the program once again, enter several student data. Lastly check local disk D, find the folder named my documents and open it. Open the file Test again and you will find all the records.

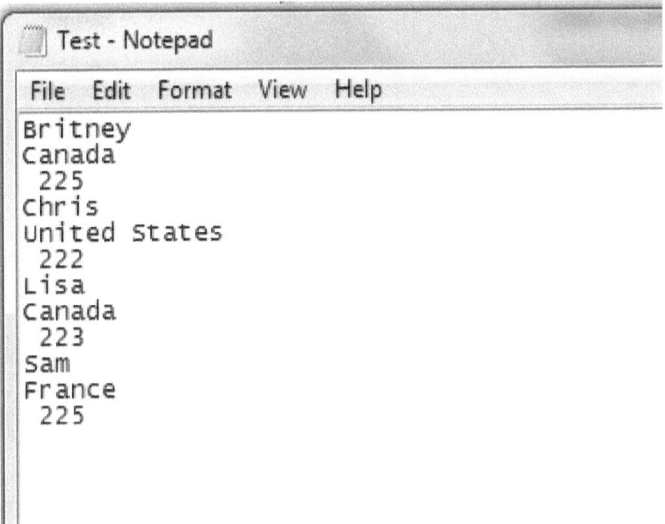

```
Test - Notepad
File  Edit  Format  View  Help
Britney
Canada
 225
chris
United States
 222
Lisa
canada
 223
Sam
France
 225
```

Reading a file

To read a file, you can use the *input* # statement. We open the file according to its file number and the variable that hold the data in it. The variable is declared using the DIM command.

For example, let's read data from the previous file. Add a command button *Cmdread* and Caption *Read File*. Double click to code.

```
Private Sub Cmdread_Click()
Dim SName, Country As String, Adm As Integer
Open "C:\My Documents\Test.txt" For Input As #1
Input #1, SName
TXTNAME.Text = SName
Input #1, Country
TxtCountry.Text = Country
Input #1, Adm
TXTADM.Text = Adm

Close #1

End Sub
```

This program opens our *Test.txt* file and displays its contents in the textboxes *Txtname, TxtCountry,* and *Txtadm.*

73

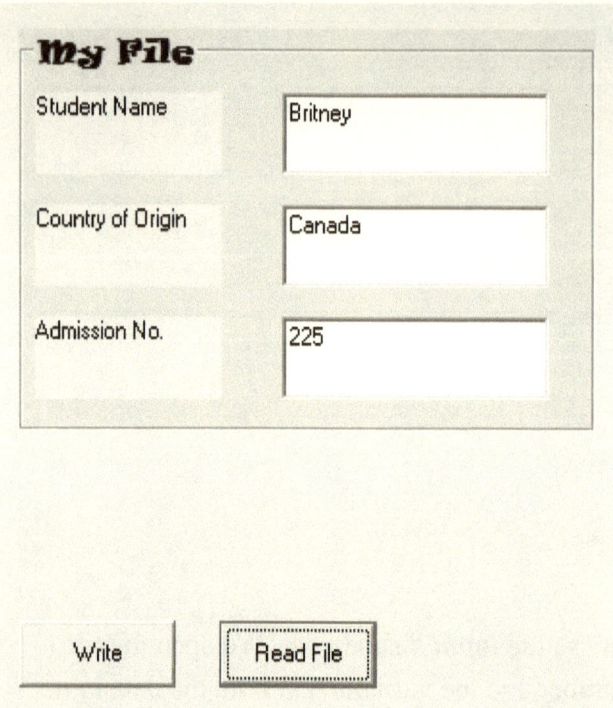

Exercise

Create and read a file with the following student information, First name, Surname, Admission number, Gender, Date of birth, Fee payable, Fee paid and Balance.

Creating Database

From the previous topic we have seen a file as a way to store information for future utilization. The most admired and powerful method is to create a **database**.

Visual Basic lets us handle databases created with different database programs such as MS Access, Oracle, MySQL and more.

ADO (ActiveX Data Object) data control

The **ADO** (ActiveX Data Object) data control is the main interface connecting a Visual Basic application and a database.

It can be used to do the following tasks:
   a.   Connecting to a database

   b.   Open a specified database table

   c.   Add fresh records or update a database

   d.   Show any errors that may occur while getting data

   e.   Close the database

Data Control Properties

Align   This property determines where data control is displayed

Caption   This is text displayed on the data control

ConnectionString   This contains the information used to establish a connection to a database

LockType   This indicates the type of locks placed on
records during

RecordSource   This determines the table which the data
control is attached to
Recordset   A set of records defined by ConnectionString
and RecordSource

One data control is required for every database table. One record is
accessible to each data control at any one time.

Data control appears with the assigned caption and four arrow
buttons.

Example 1

Write a simple program to calculate the area of a rectangle and link
it to a Ms Access database.

Let's start by creating the user interface. Open form as usual and
arrange the controls. Add commands *Add New*, *Save*, *Previous*,
Next, *Last* and *delete Record*. Also add a datagrid Control. This is
used to display the contents from the database table. Data control
and datagrid control are not available in the Visual Basic toolbox. To
use them, select *Project* from the main menu, then click
Components.

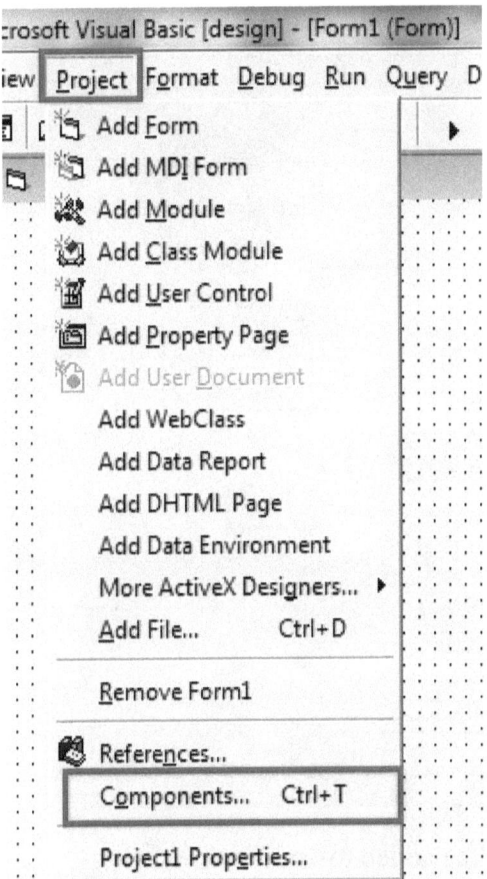

From the Components window, check *Microsoft ADO Data Control*, and then click Apply then OK.

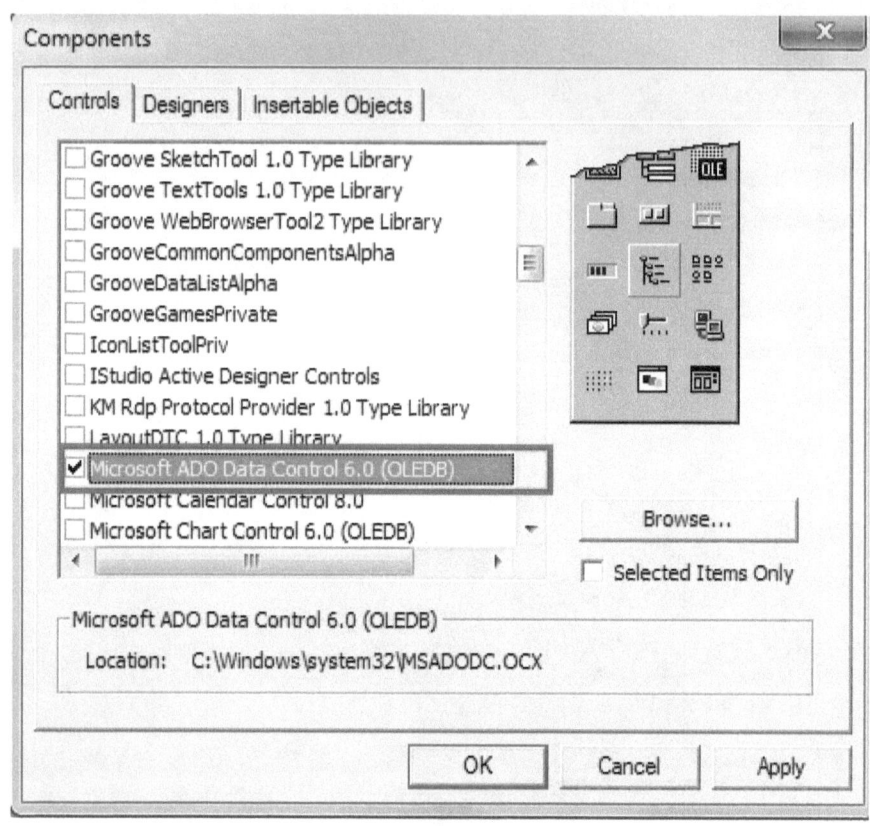

The The Active Data control will be added to your toolbox.

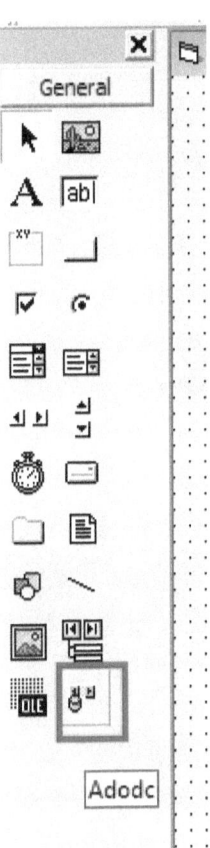

For Datagrid control check Microsoft DataGrid Control 6.0
(OLEBD)

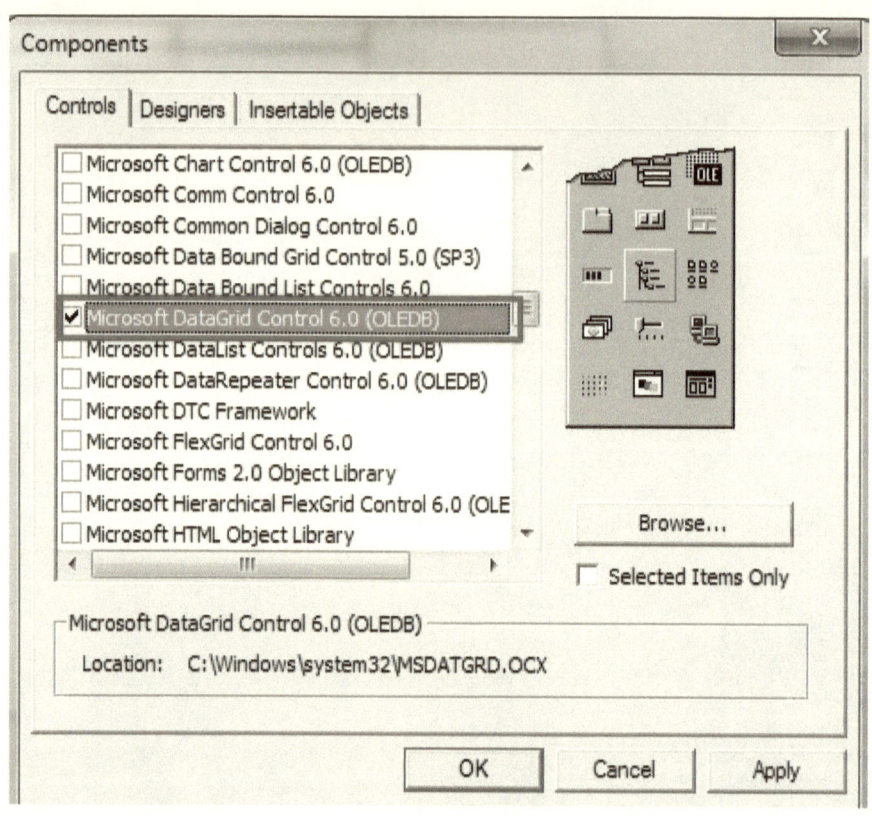

The DataGrid control will be added to your toolbox.

Arrange the controls on the form to bring a nice interface.

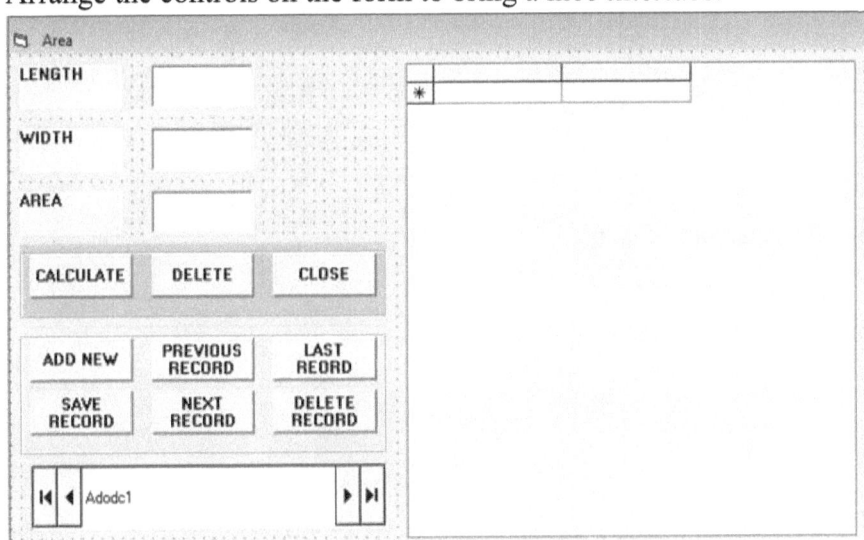

To code command **Calculate:**

```
Private Sub CMDCALC_Click()
If TXTLENGTH.Text = "" Then
MsgBox "Please enter your Length"
ElseIf Not IsNumeric(TXTLENGTH.Text) Then
MsgBox "Only Numbers are allowed"
TXTLENGTH.Text = ""
TXTLENGTH.SetFocus
ElseIf TXTWIDTH.Text = "" Then
MsgBox "Please enter your Length"
ElseIf Not IsNumeric(TXTWIDTH.Text) Then
MsgBox "Only numbers are allowed"
TXTWIDTH.Text = ""
TXTWIDTH.SetFocus
End If
TXTAREA.Text = Val(TXTLENGTH.Text) * Val(TXTWIDTH.Text)

End Sub
```

To code command **Add New:**

```
Private Sub CMDAdd_Click()
Adodc1.Recordset.AddNew
TXTLENGTH.SetFocus

End Sub
```

To code command **Save**

```
Private Sub CmdSave_Click()
Adodc1.Recordset.Update
CMDAdd.Enabled = True

End Sub
```

To code command **Previous:**

```
Private Sub CMDPrevious_Click()
If Not (Adodc1.Recordset.BOF) Then
Adodc1.Recordset.MovePrevious
Else
Adodc1.Recordset.MoveFirst
End If

End Sub
```

To code command **Next:**

```
Private Sub CmdNext_Click()
If Adodc1.Recordset.EOF Then
Adodc1.Recordset.MoveLast
Else
Adodc1.Recordset.MoveNext
End If

End Sub
```

To code command **Last Record:**

```
Private Sub CMDLast_Click()
Adodc1.Recordset.MoveLast

End Sub
```

To code command **Delete Record:**

```
Private Sub CMDDelete_Click()
If MsgBox("Do you want to delete the record???", vbYesNo, "Delete") = vbYes Then
Adodc1.Recordset.Delete
Else
MsgBox "Record not deleted"
End If

End Sub
```

Exercise

Code commands *Delete* and *Close*

Linking the Area program to the Ms access Database

After creating the Graphical user interface and the codes, let's start linking the program to the database. First save the program.

Open a blank Ms Access database and give it a name.

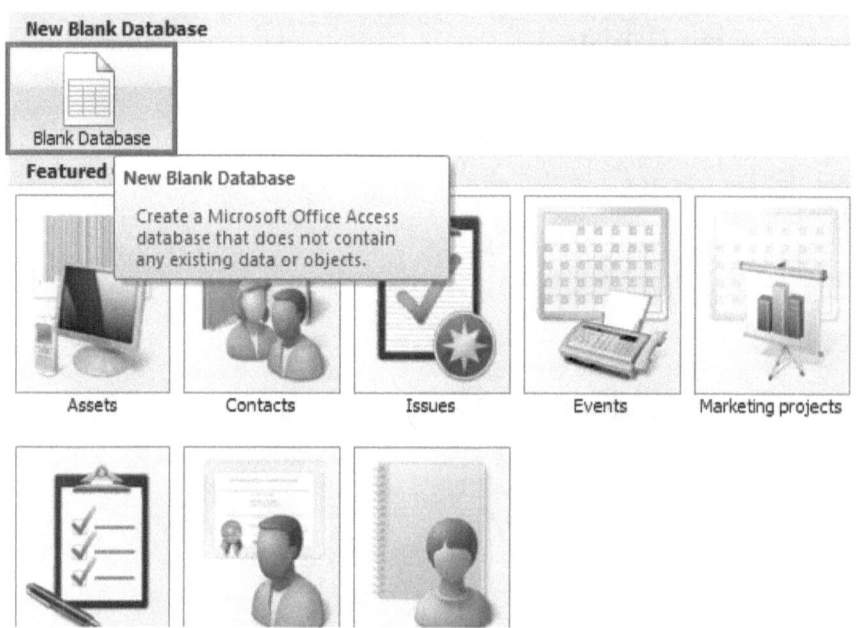

Blank Database

Create a Microsoft Office Access database that does not contain any existing data or objects.

File Name:

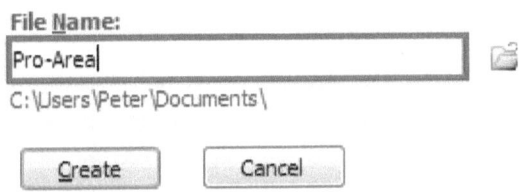

Pro-Area

C:\Users\Peter\Documents\

[Create]   [Cancel]

In this case I decided to name it *Pro-Area*. Click Create.

Right click Table 1 and choose **Design View**

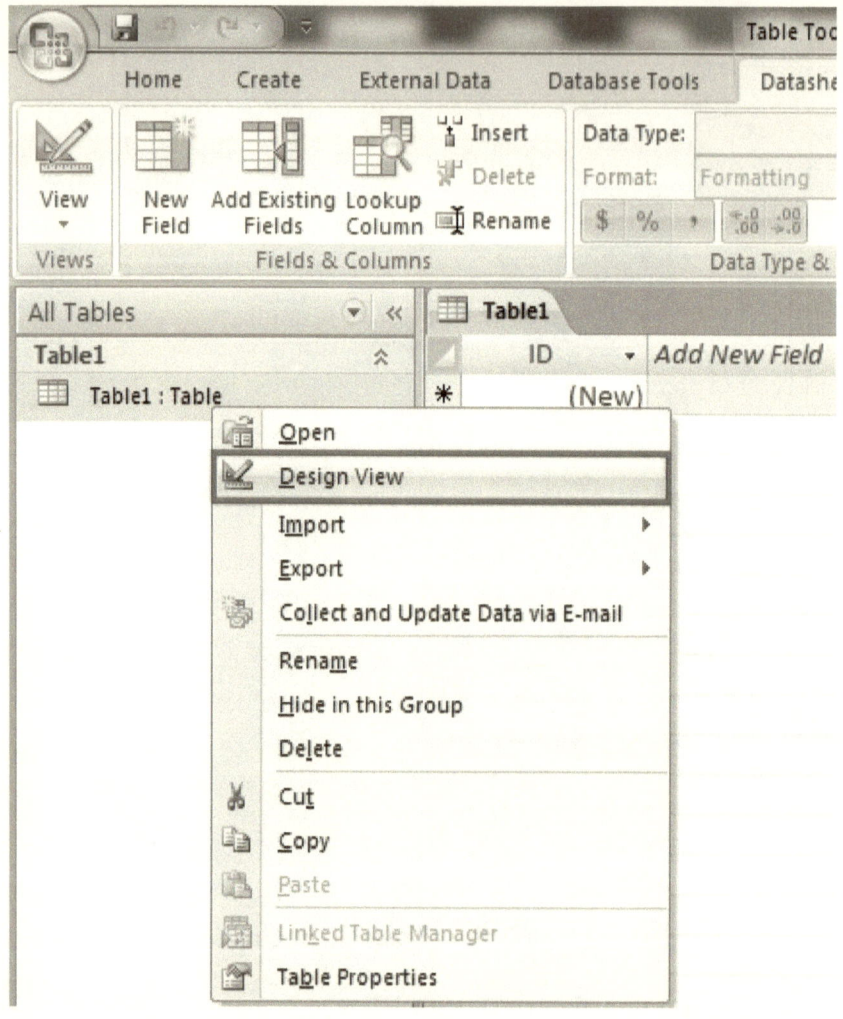

Give the table a name. In this example am naming it area.

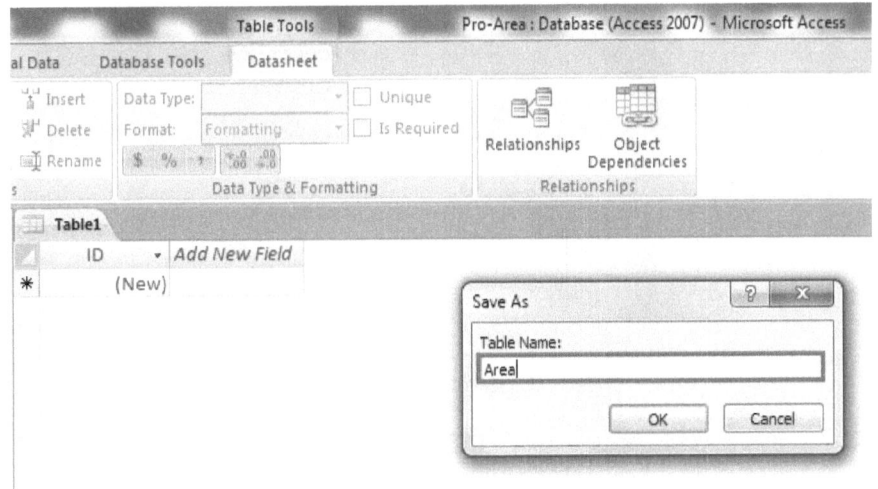

Enter the three fields that is Length, Width and Area and choose their data types.

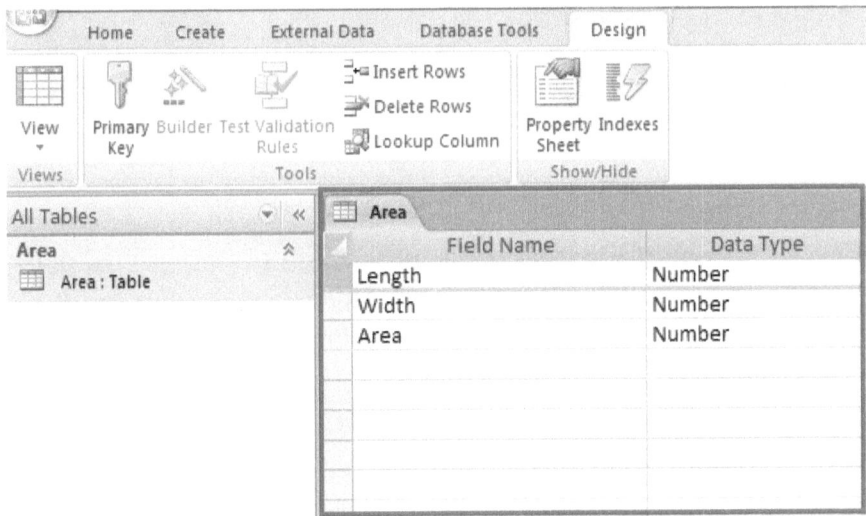

Close the table and save changes.

Lastly save the database. Click **Office Button**, point **Save As** and choose **Access 2000-2003 Database** format.

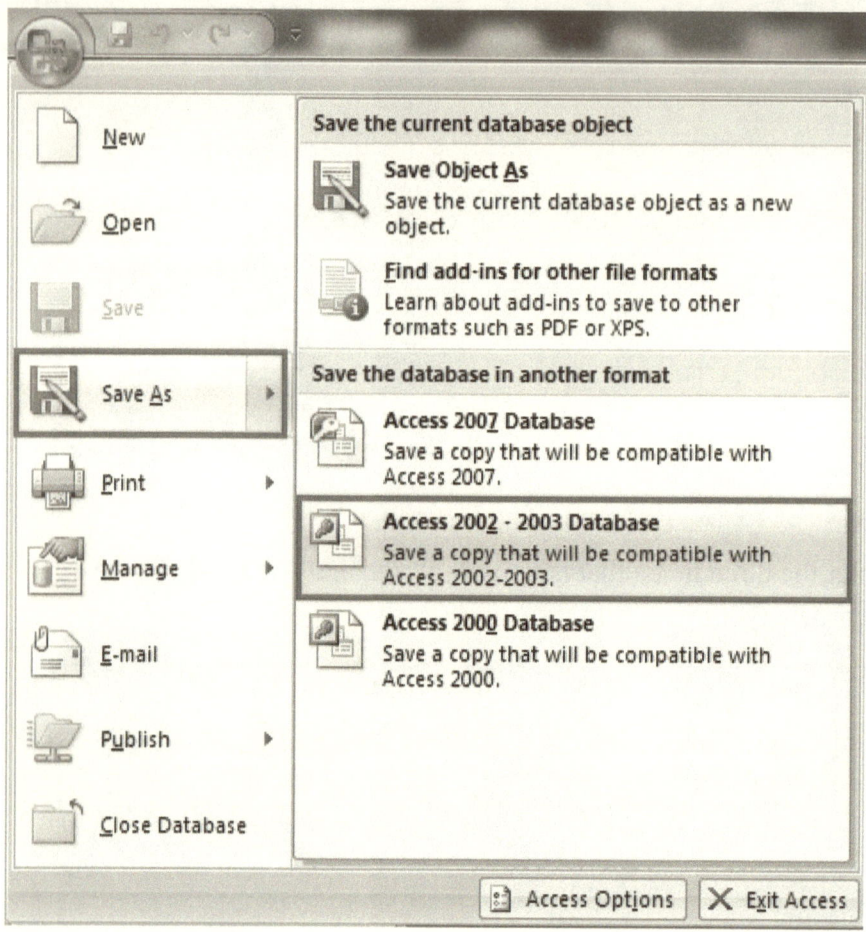

Save it on the same folder as our project. This will make it easier for us to move the program and its database to another computer without a problem.

Note that we have named the database ***Pro-Area*** and the table as ***Area***.

Now let's go back to the Area program

Click on Active data object (Adodc1) and on Properties window click **Connection String**, this contains the information used to establish a connection to a database.

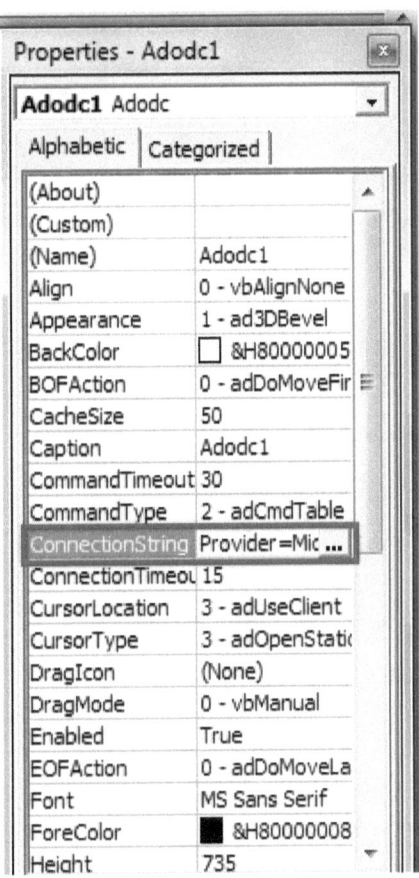

On **property Pages** choose the option **Use connection String** and click **Build**.

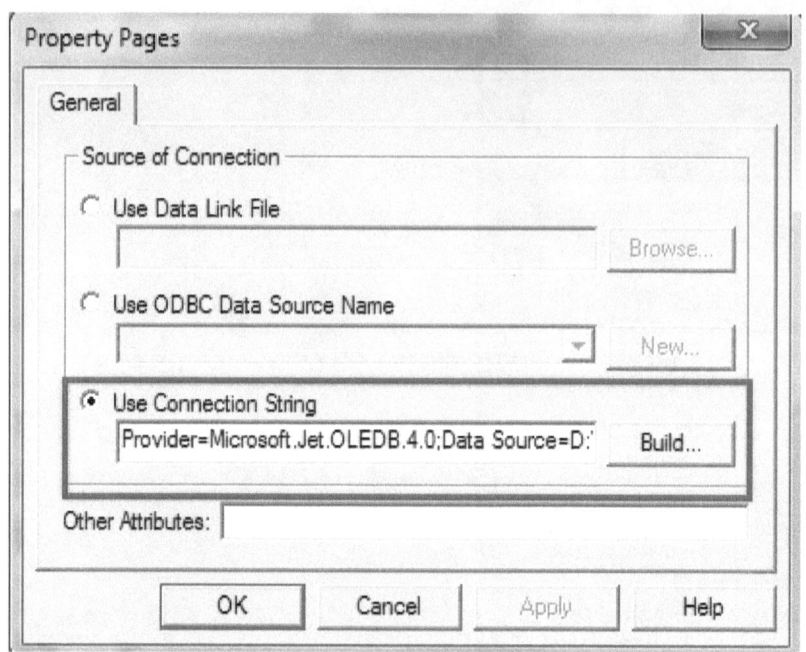

Choose the database. In this example am choosing our database *Pro-Area*.

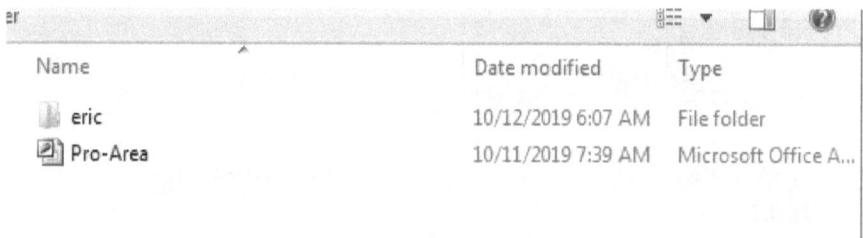

Click **Open**. Click **Test Connection**.

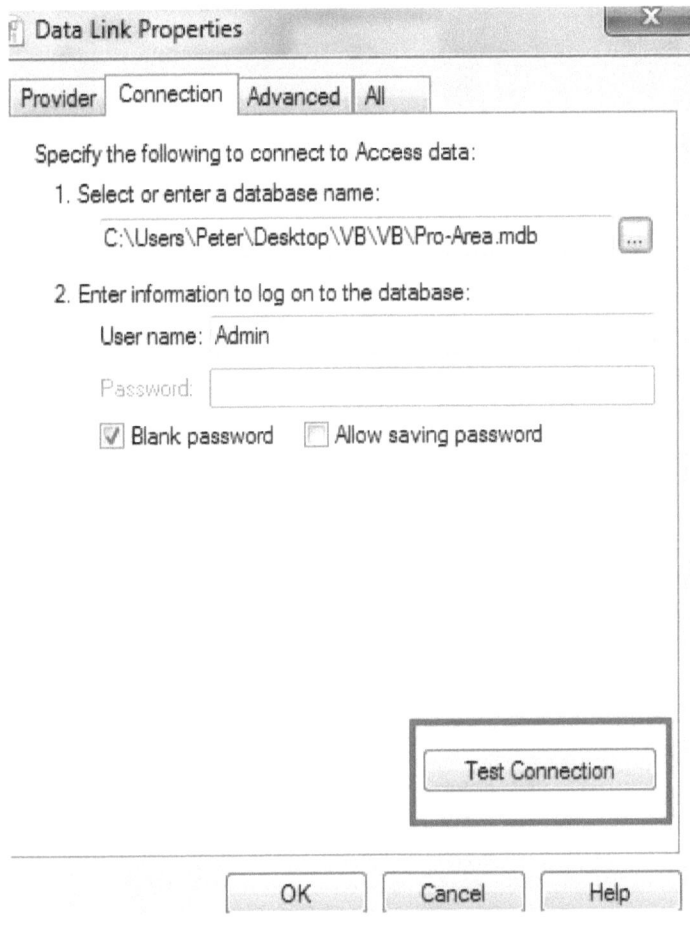

A message box with **"Test Connection Succeed"** must appear for one to continue.

Click **Ok**, then click **Apply** then **Ok**.

Now the connection to the database is okay. Next we link the database table.

Click on Active data object (Adodc1) and on Properties window click **RecordSource**, this determines the table which the data control is attached to.

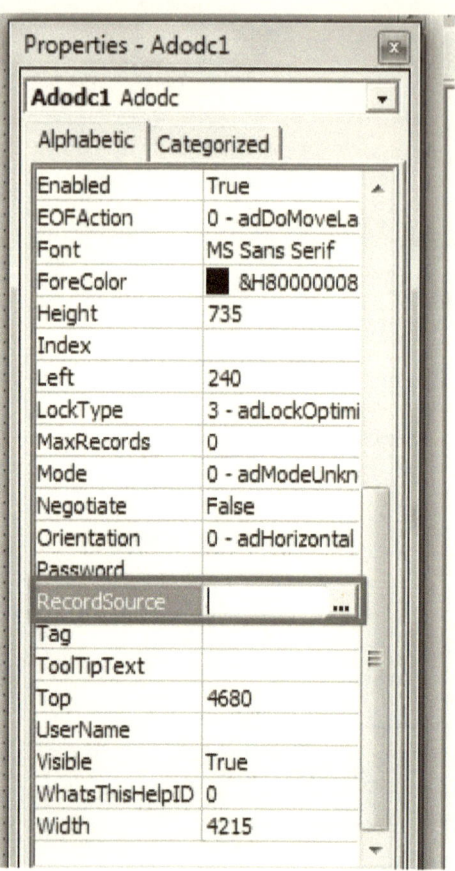

On **property Pages** choose 2-adCmdTable under **Command Type** and then choose the table name under **Table or Stored Procedure Name**. In this example I can find our table *area*.

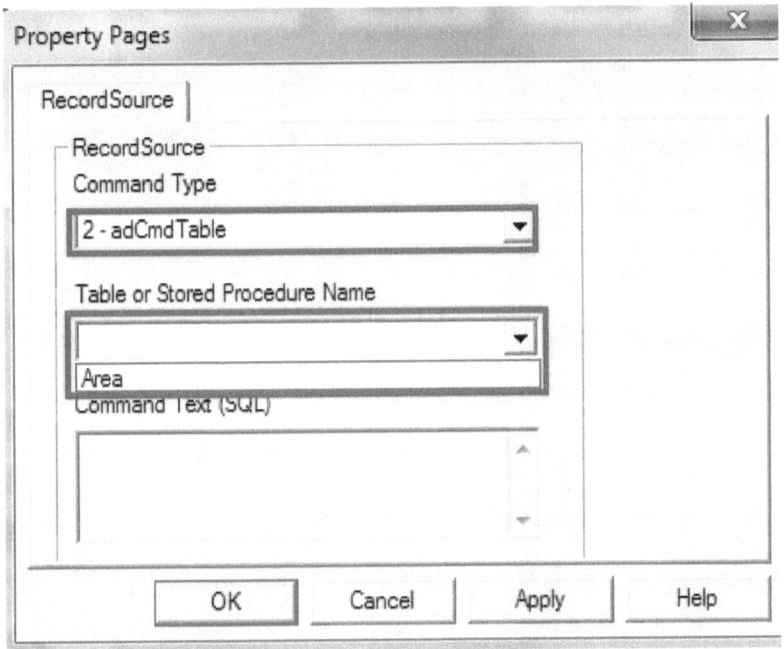

Click Apply then Ok. Our table is now linked.

Lastly we look at **Recordset,** It isa set of records defined by
ConnectionString and **RecordSource**. Click on first data input
control, in this example it is textbox **length** and on Properties
window I click **Datasource**, on the datasource pulldown I choose
Adodc1. This is our data control.

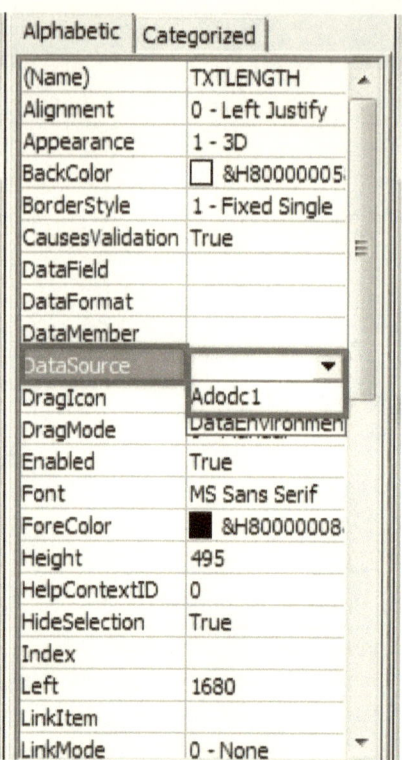

Click on DataField property and choose the preferred record from the database table. In this example am going for **Length**.

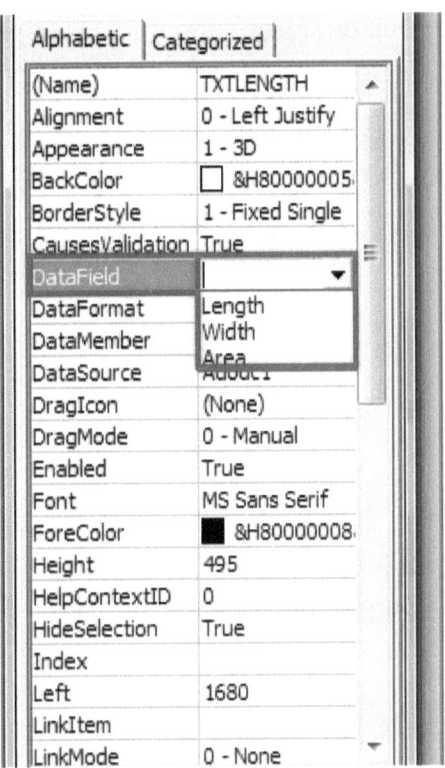

Alphabetic	Categorized
(Name)	TXTLENGTH
Alignment	0 - Left Justify
Appearance	1 - 3D
BackColor	&H80000005
BorderStyle	1 - Fixed Single
CausesValidation	True
DataField	
DataFormat	Length
DataMember	Width
DataSource	Area Adodc1
DragIcon	(None)
DragMode	0 - Manual
Enabled	True
Font	MS Sans Serif
ForeColor	&H80000008
Height	495
HelpContextID	0
HideSelection	True
Index	
Left	1680
LinkItem	
LinkMode	0 - None

Repeat this procedure for all the other controls, that is **datasource** choose Adodc1, datafield choose **Width**, for area we choose Adodc1 as **datasource** and **Area** as **dataField**.

To link datagrid to the database table, click datagrid control, and on Properties window click **Datasource** and select Adodc1. For both

95

properties Allow **Addnew** and **AllowDelete**, select True.

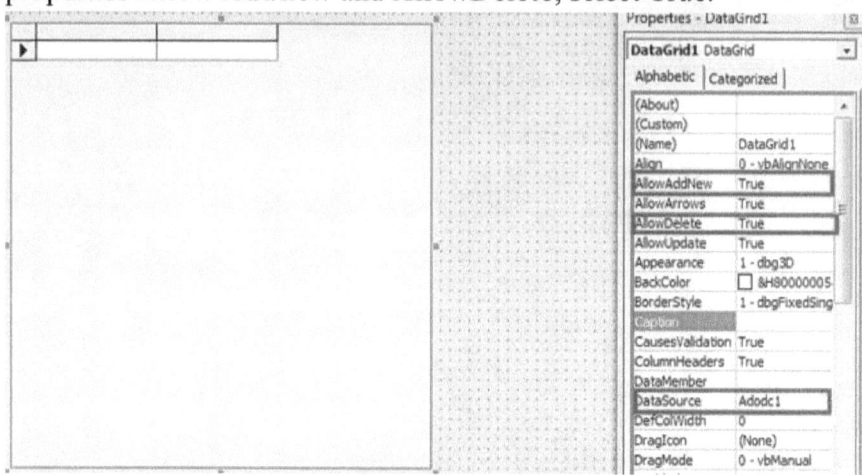

Run the program, click command **Add New**, enter length, width then click command **calculate**. This will give the area. Finally click command **Save Record**.

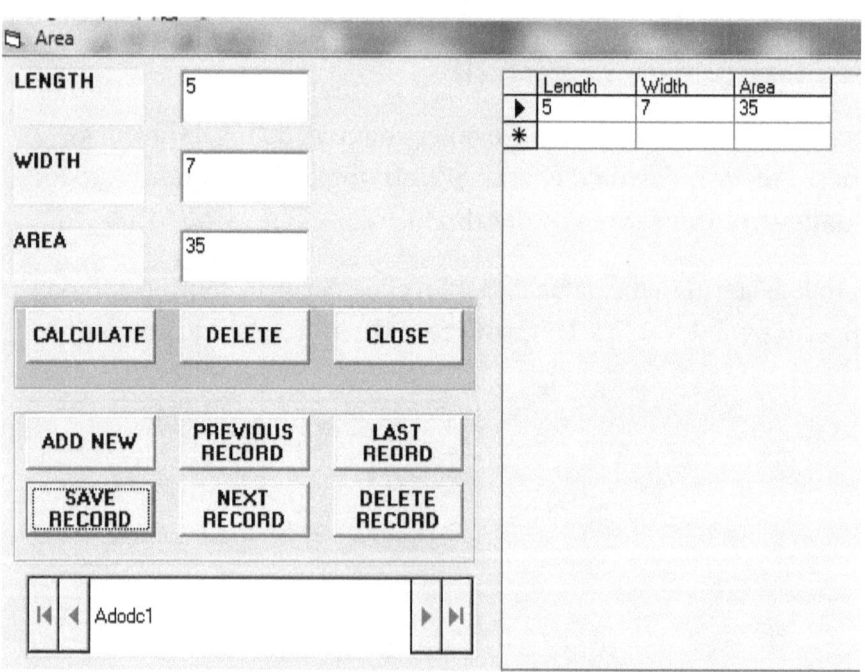

Enter more measurements and see how the Datagrid looks like. Remember to click Add New, enter the records, click Calculate and Save the record.

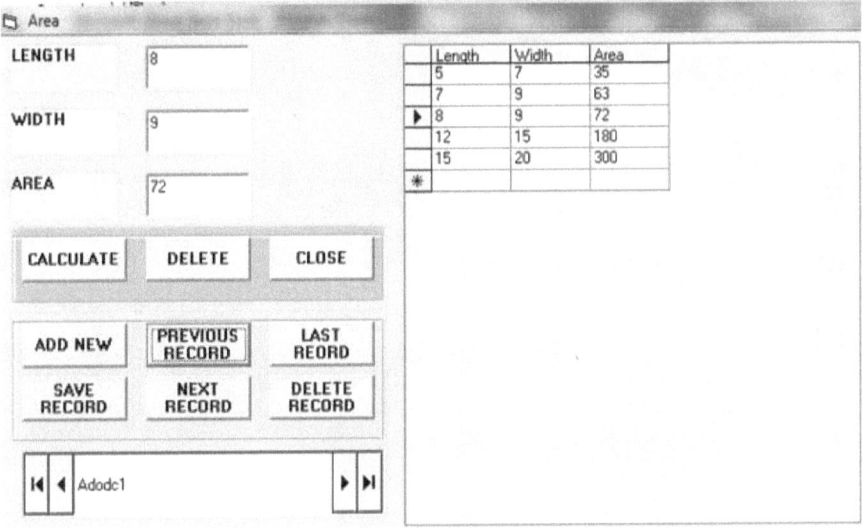

Try other commands. Am trying command Delete Record.

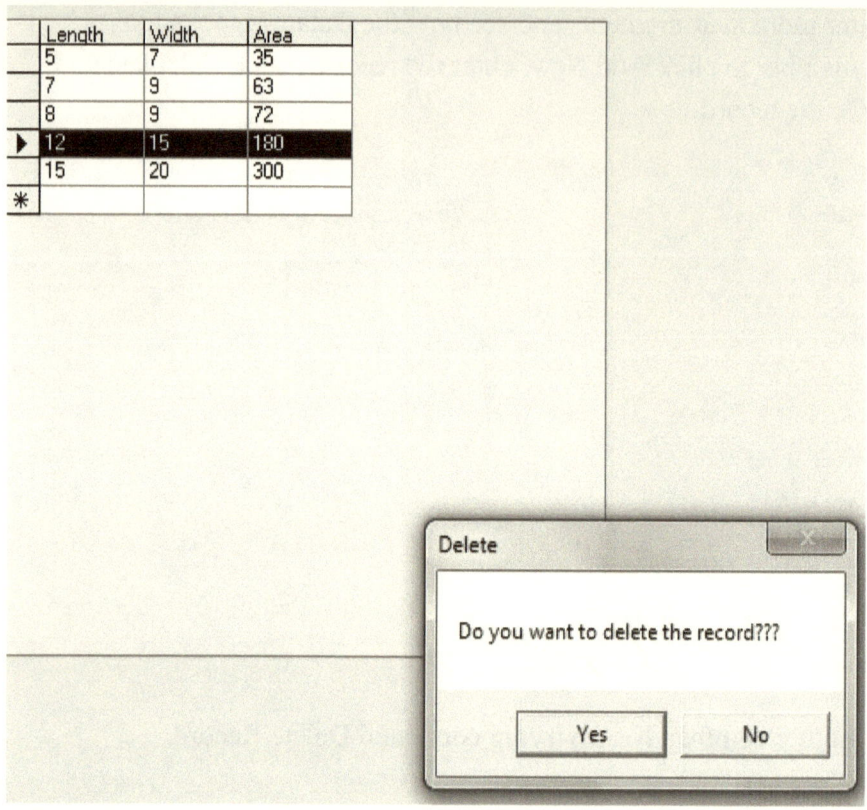

Example 2

Create a payroll form with the following interface, and link it to Ms
Access database:

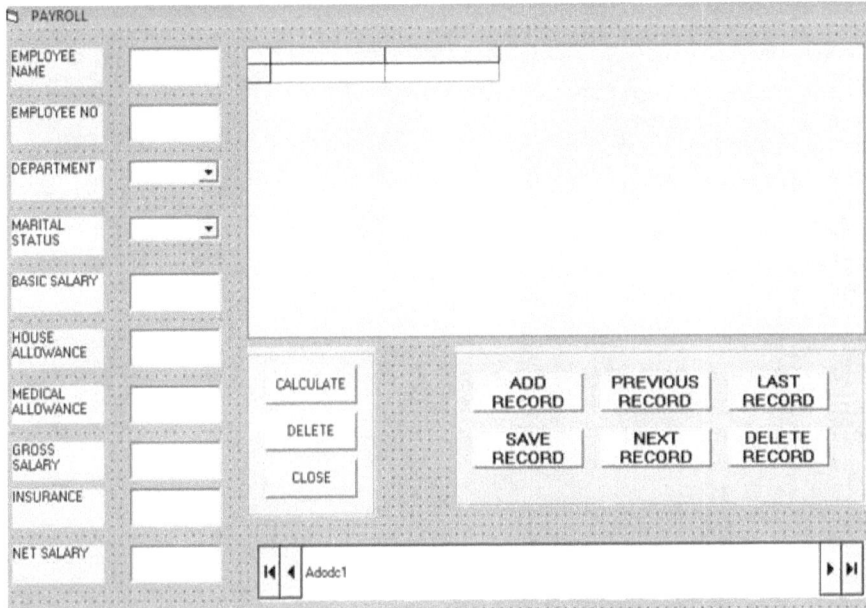

Coding the command Calculate:

```
Private Sub CMDCALC_Click()

Select Case CboDepartment.Text
Case Is = "Computer"
TxtBasicsal = 15000
Case Is = "Sales"
TxtBasicsal = 12000
Case Is = "Purchases"
TxtBasicsal = 25000
Case Is = "Accounts"
TxtBasicsal = 20500
End Select
Select Case CboDepartment.Text
Case Is = "Computer"
TxtHouse = 2.5 / 10 * 15000
Case Is = "Sales"
TxtHouse = 1.7 / 100 * 12000
Case Is = "Purchases"
TxtHouse = 3 / 100 * 25000
Case Is = "Accounts"
TxtHouse = 3.2 / 100 * 20500
End Select
TxtMedical = 2 / 100 * Val(TxtBasicsal)
TxtGross = Val(TxtBasicsal) + Val(TxtHouse) + Val(TxtMedical)
Select Case CboStatus.Text
Case Is = "Single"
TXTINSURE = 200
Case Is = "Married"
TXTINSURE = 300
End Select
TXTNETSALARY = Val(TxtGross) - Val(TXTINSURE)

End Sub
```

Coding the command Add Record:

```
Private Sub CmdAdd_Click()
Adodc1.Recordset.AddNew
TXTEMPNAME.SetFocus

End Sub
```

Coding the command Save Record:

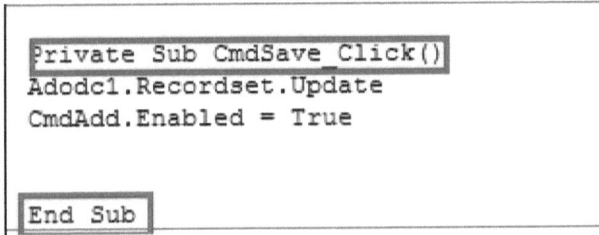

```
Private Sub CmdSave_Click()
Adodc1.Recordset.Update
CmdAdd.Enabled = True

End Sub
```

Exercise

Code commands *Delete, Close, Previous Record, Next Record, Last Record and Delete Record.*

Let's proceed to the Ms Access database. First we create a database *Employee* with a table called *Payroll*. Save as Access *2002-2003 Database*.

Next, we go back to the vb project and start connection to this database using **connection string** property and select **Employee** database.

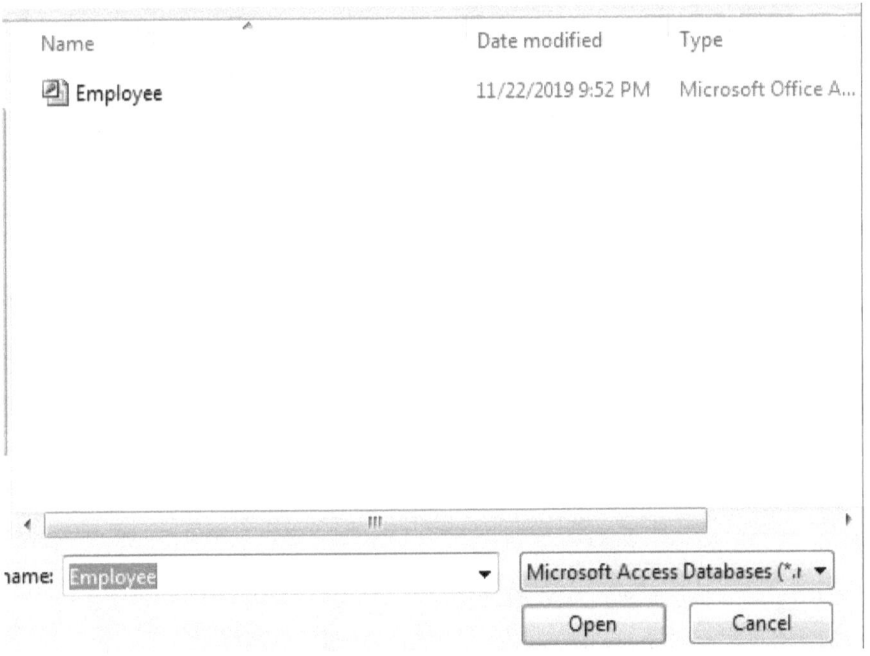

Using property **Record source** we select table **payroll**.

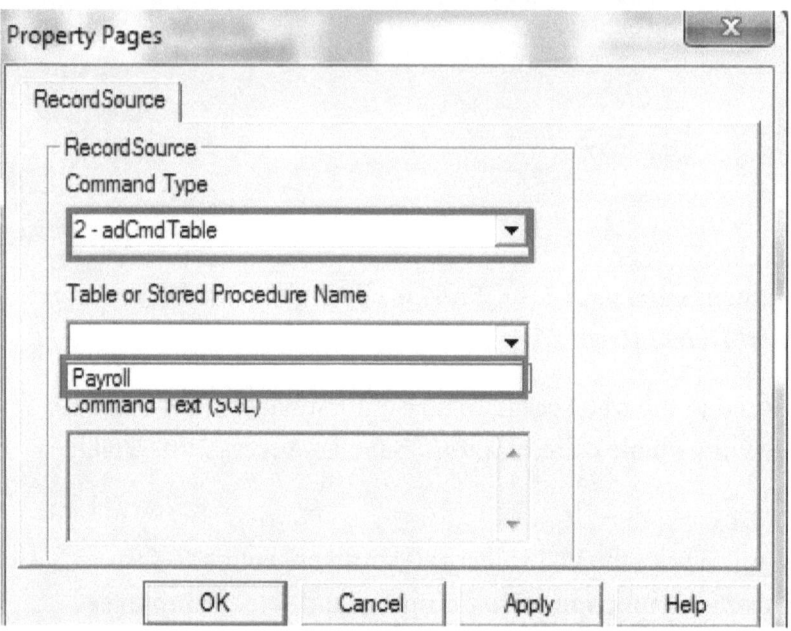

Select each of the input controls, i.e Textboxes and combo boxes and on DataSource property select Adodc1 and DataField property, select the respective field from the database. For example for Employee name textbox select field Employee name

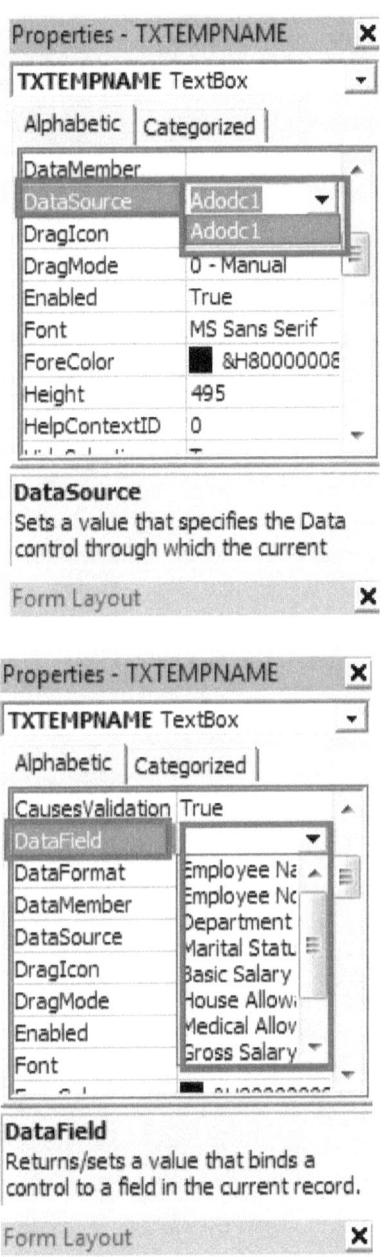

Remember to link the datagrid control. Select DataGrid control, on properties window, set property **DataSource** as **Adodc1** and **Allow**

Addnew as ***True***.

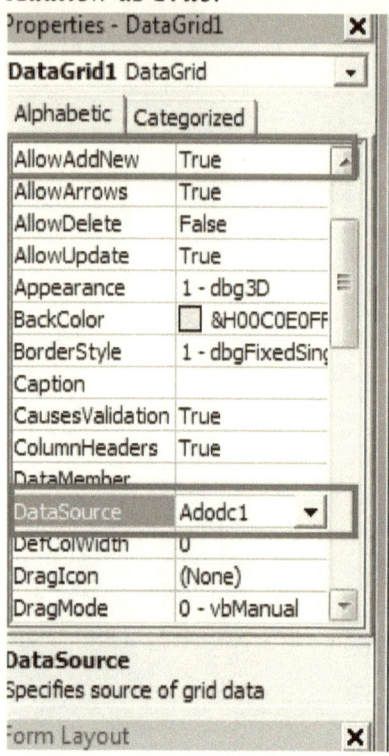

Lastly we run the program, click command **Add Record**, enter the required information and click command **Save Record**. We expect to get the entered data on our database.

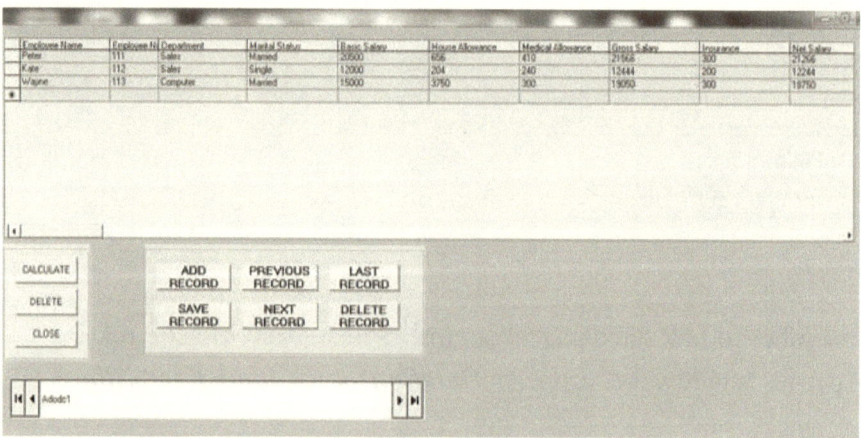

Exercise

Create a water account application form with the following
Graphical User Interface and connect it to Ms Access database.

Creating a Data Report

This is the process of obtaining a printed or hard copy of Visual basic information from the database.

This is done in two steps. The first step we need a **Data Environment**. The Data Environment is used to connect the data report with the database. Second, we need the **Data Report**. The **Data Environment** and **Data Report** files then happen to be part of the Visual Basic project developed as a database management system.

Example

Using our previous database called *Employee*, we will create a data report by first creating a Data Environment, then a Data Report.

Creating a Data Environment

Open our previous project, **Payroll**

Click on the **Project** menu and choose **Add Data Environment**

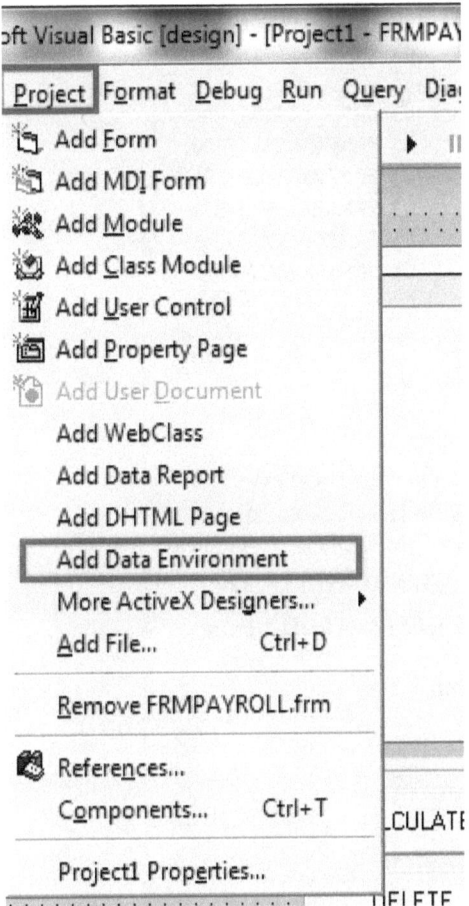

Alternatively, you can right click project explorer, choose **Add** then choose **Data environment**

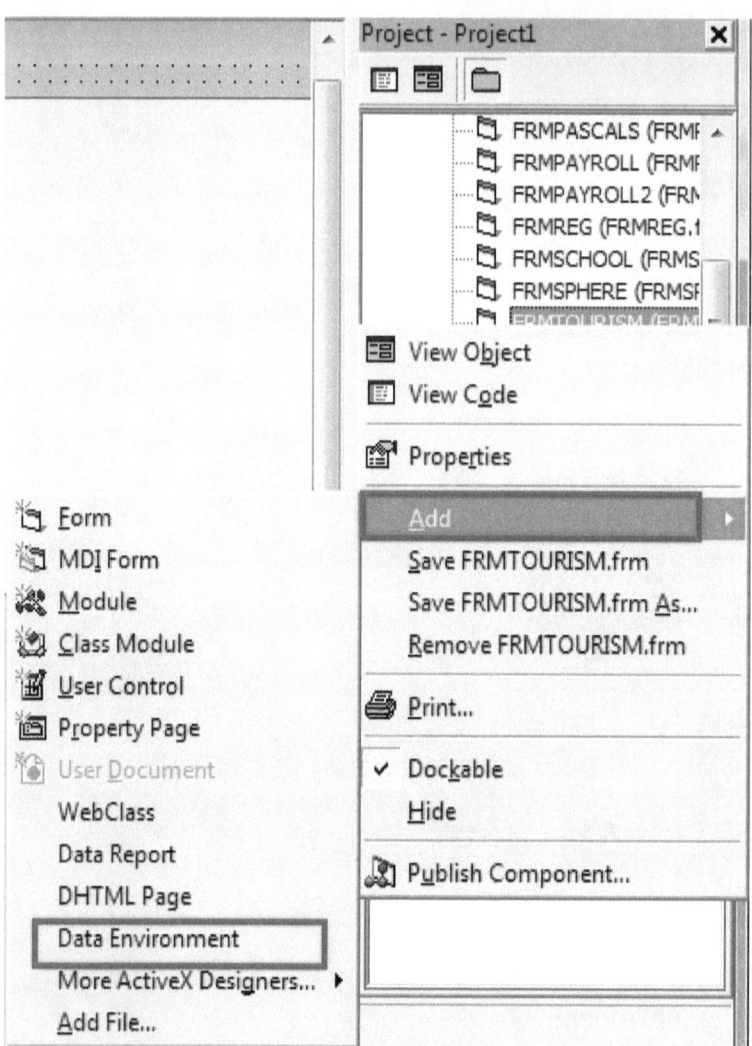

This is where we point to our database. In the Data Environment window, right-click the **Connection1** tab and select **Properties**.

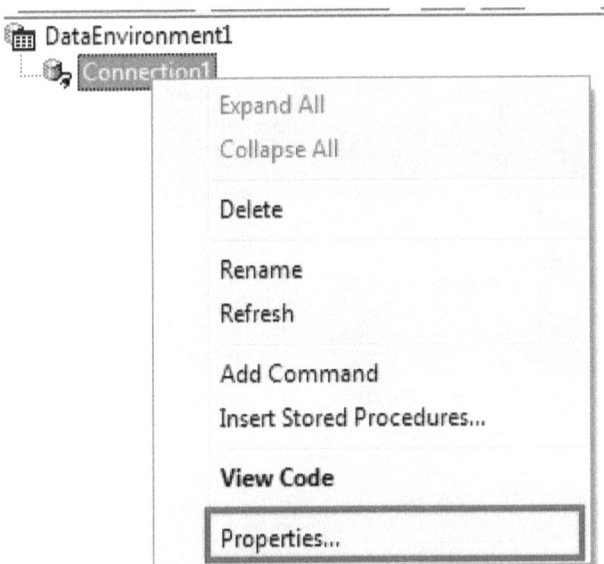

DataEnvironment1
    Connection1

Expand All
Collapse All
Delete
Rename
Refresh
Add Command
Insert Stored Procedures...
View Code
Properties...

In the ***Data Link Properties*** dialog box, choose Microsoft Jet 4.0
OLE DB Provider.

Click ***Next***

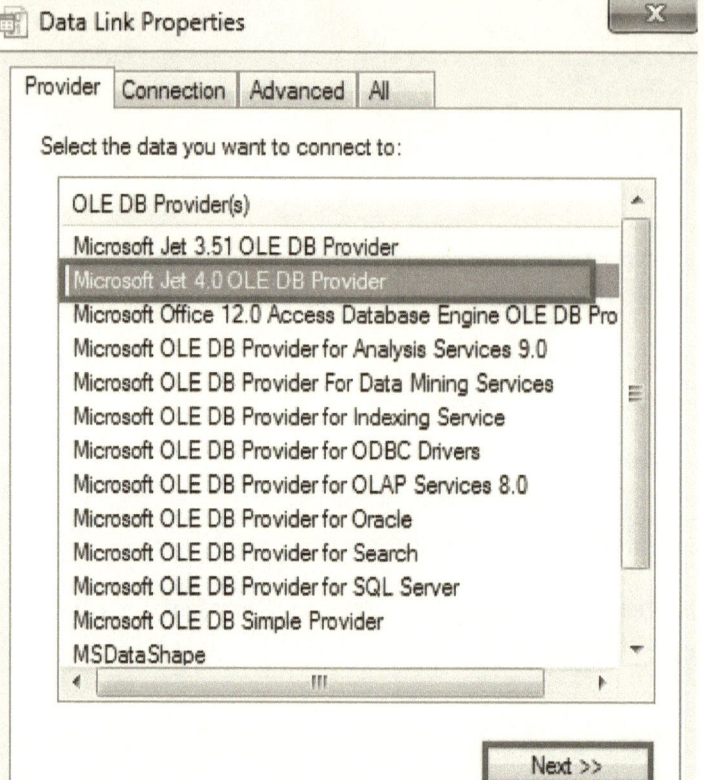

Select or enter database name.

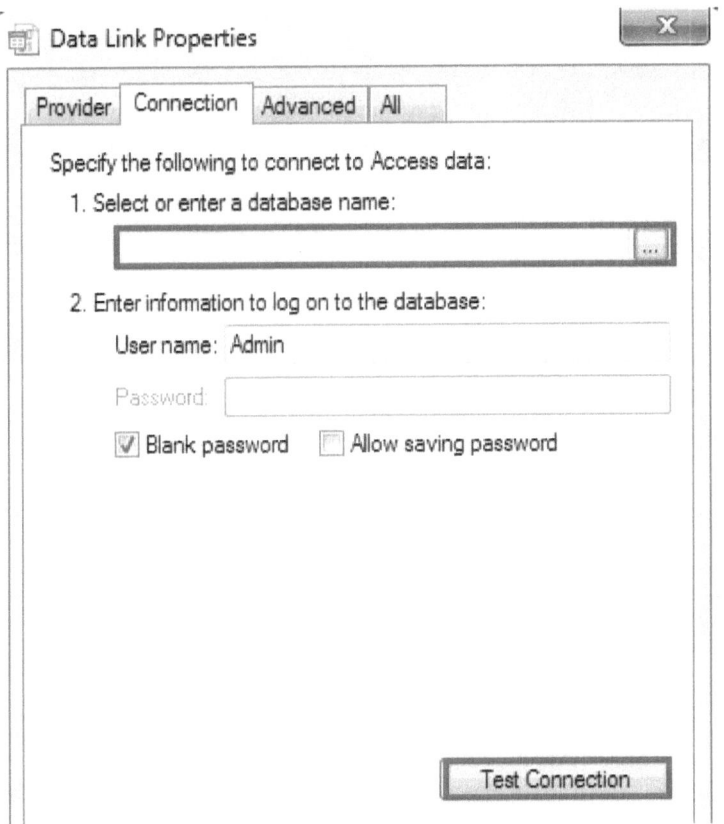

Data Link Properties

Provider | Connection | Advanced | All

Specify the following to connect to Access data:

1. Select or enter a database name:

[   ] [...]

2. Enter information to log on to the database:

User name: Admin

Password: [   ]

☑ Blank password   ☐ Allow saving password

[Test Connection]

I this case I select our database *Employee*.

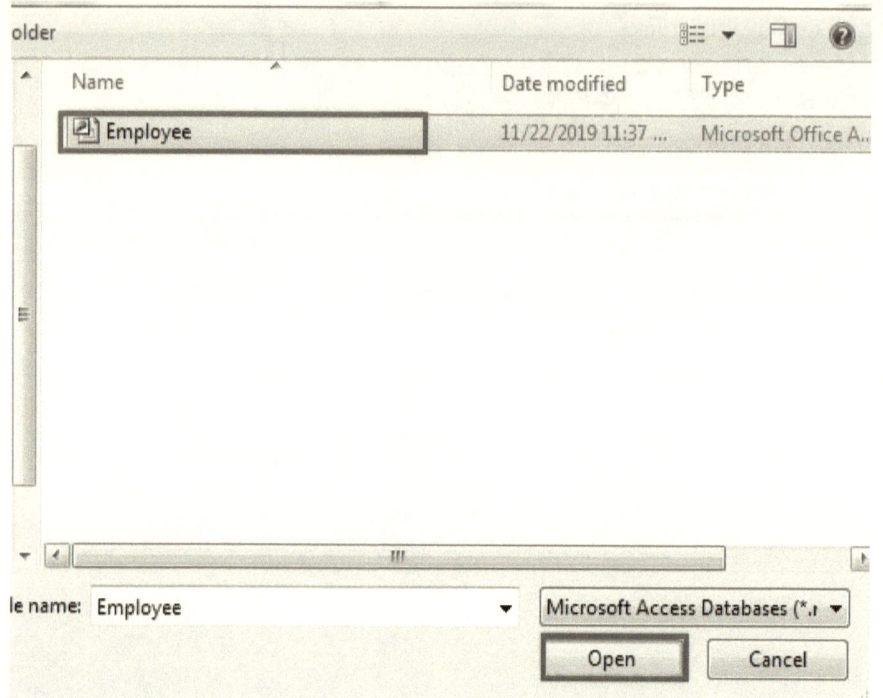

Click open. Remember to test connection

Right-click the Connection1 tab and click Add Command.

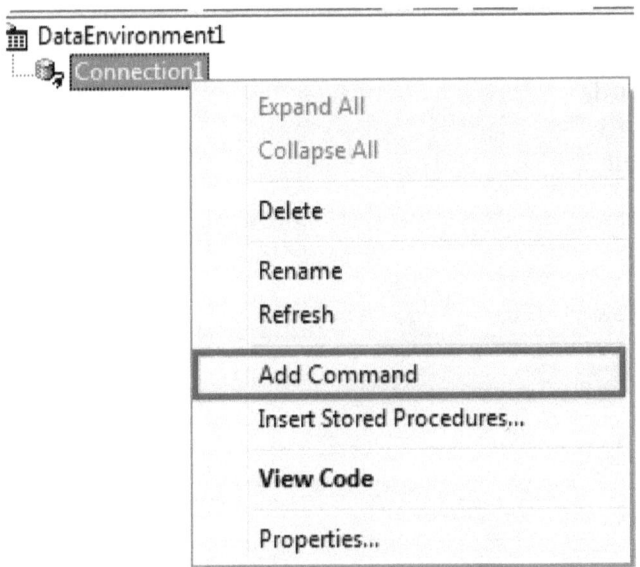

Right-click **Command1** and choose **Properties**.

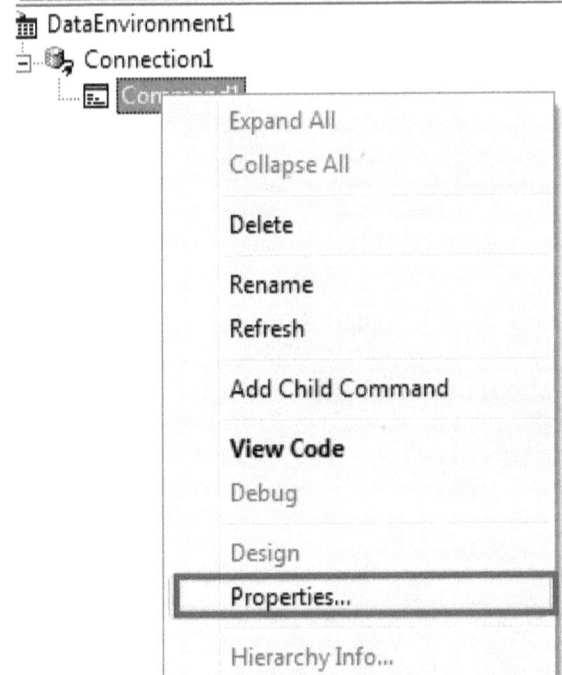

Assign the following properties:

DataBase Object - **Table**

ObjectName – **Payroll**

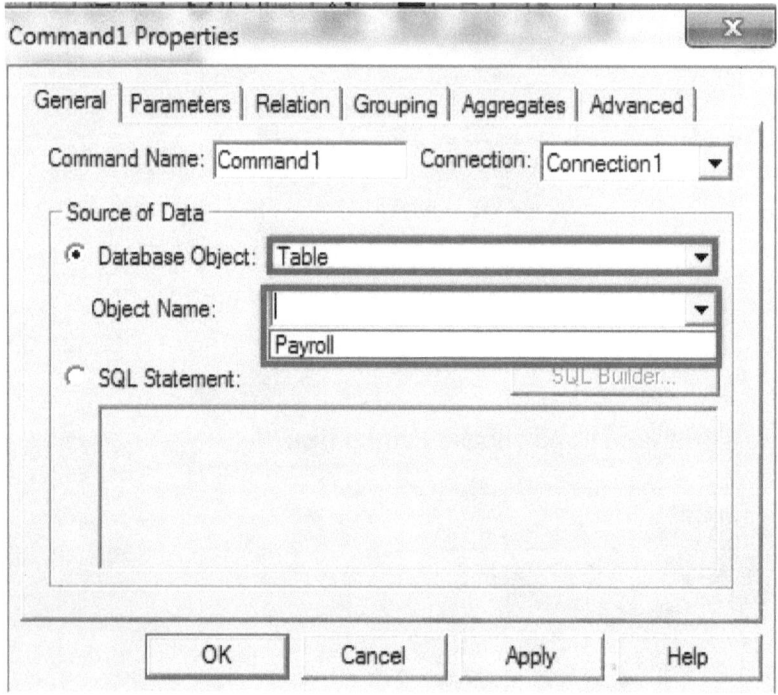

Click **Apply** and then **Ok**

The Data environment connection to the database is now successful

Right click Command1 and choose Expand All

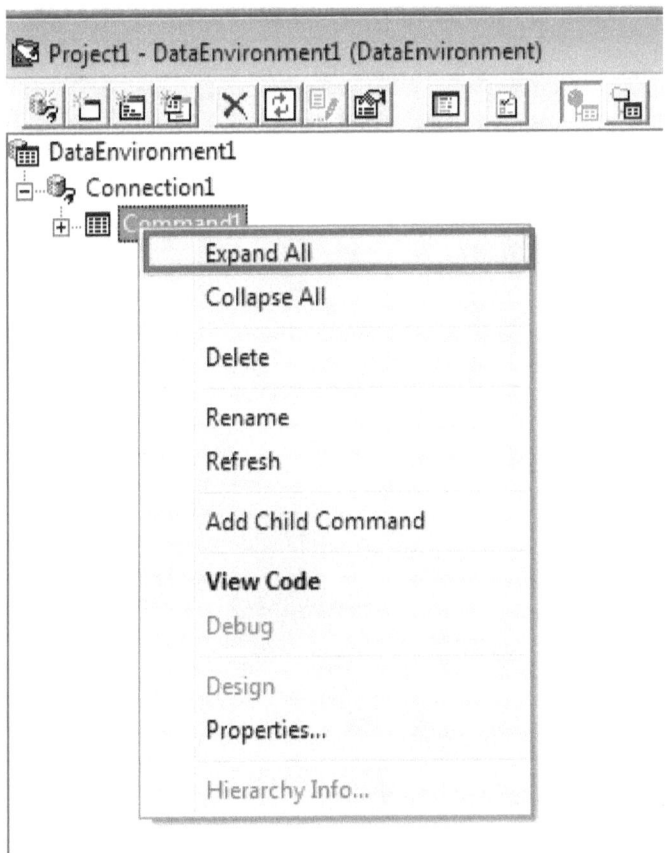

This will give us the fields from our database table

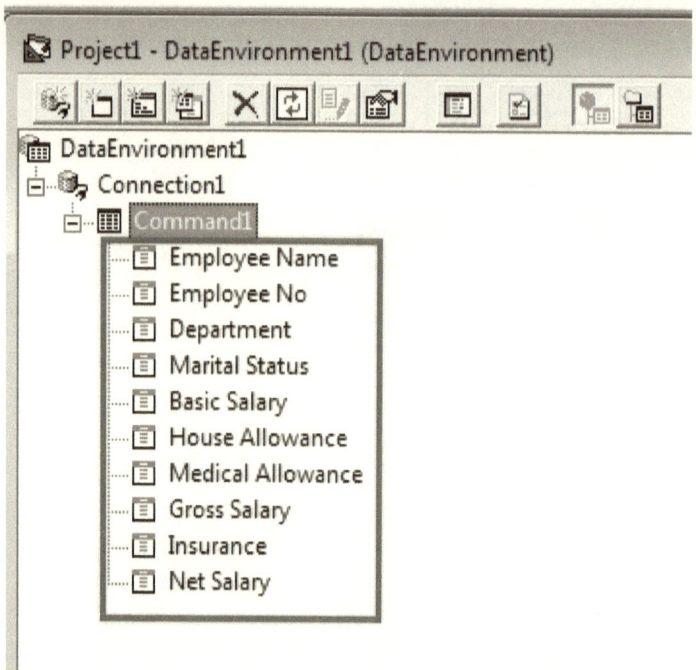

NB Remember to save the environment

Let's proceed to **creating a Data Report**

We will need to drag data out of the Data Environment onto a Data Report.

On the Project menu, click **Add Data Report** and one will be added to your project.

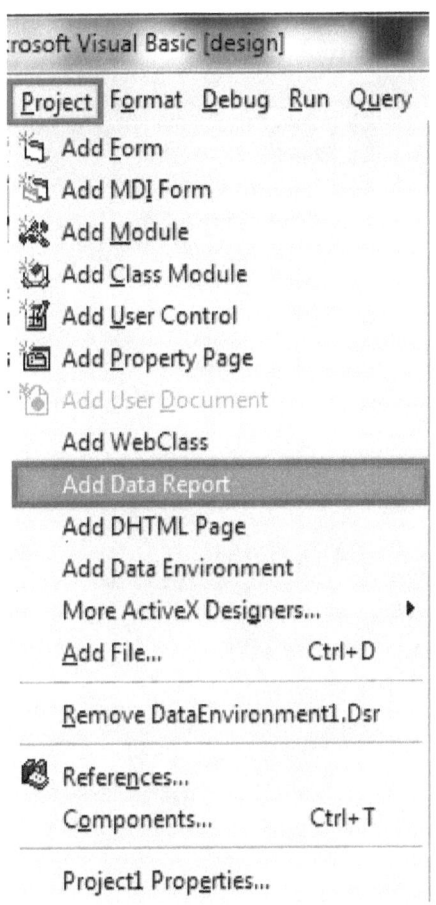

Alternatively, you can right click project explorer, choose **Add** then choose **Data Report**

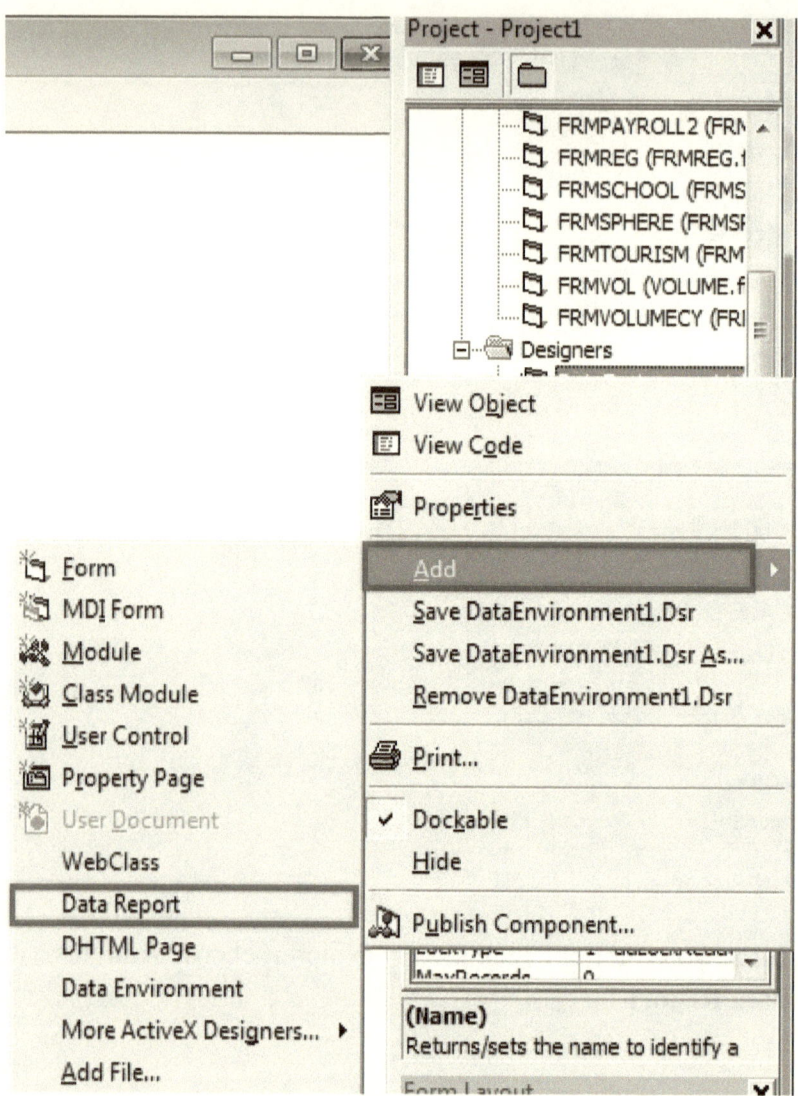

This will add a data report.

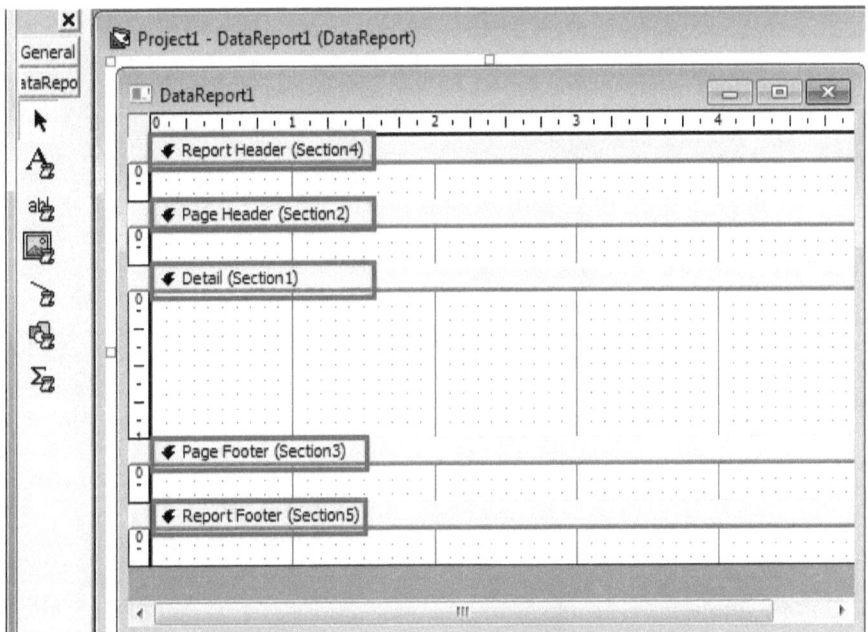

There are sections on the data report: a **Report Header**, a **Page Header**, a **Detail section**, a **Page Footer**, and a **Report Footer**. The headers and footers include information printed in the report and on each page. To put information in one of these sections, right-click the selected section, click Add Control, then choose the control you desire to use. For example we can use a label to give header or a footer and line control to separate various controls.

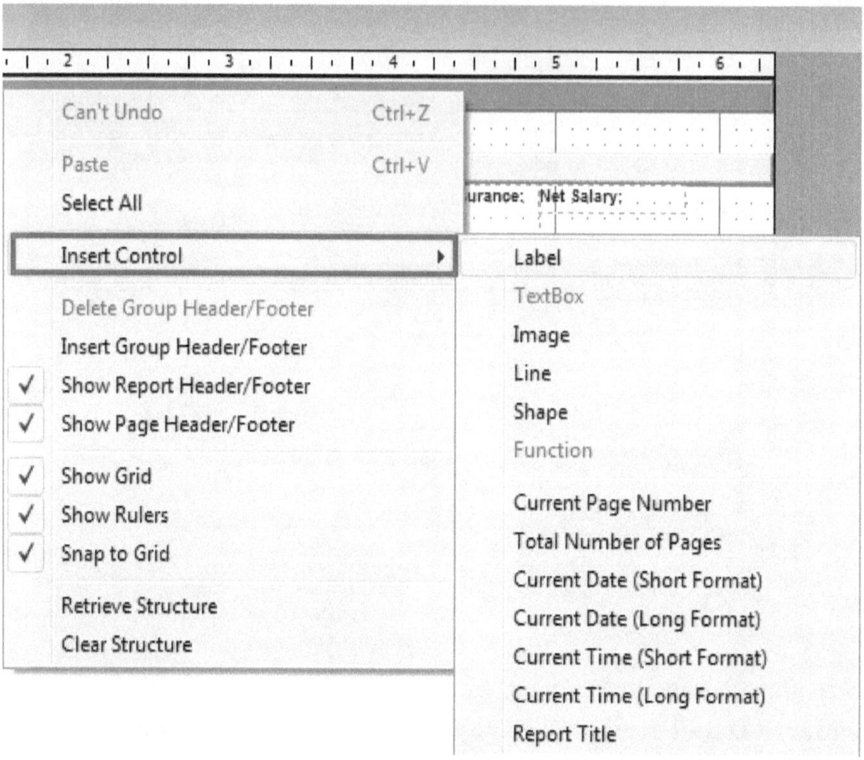

Can't Undo	Ctrl+Z	
Paste	Ctrl+V	
Select All		
Insert Control	▶	Label
Delete Group Header/Footer		TextBox
Insert Group Header/Footer		Image
✓ Show Report Header/Footer		Line
✓ Show Page Header/Footer		Shape
		Function
✓ Show Grid		
✓ Show Rulers		Current Page Number
✓ Snap to Grid		Total Number of Pages
		Current Date (Short Format)
Retrieve Structure		Current Date (Long Format)
Clear Structure		Current Time (Short Format)
		Current Time (Long Format)
		Report Title

Click on **Windows** menu and choose **Tile Horizontally**. This will give us all the forms on the project. Here we want the data report, so close all the other forms except **DataEnvironment** and **DataReport1**.

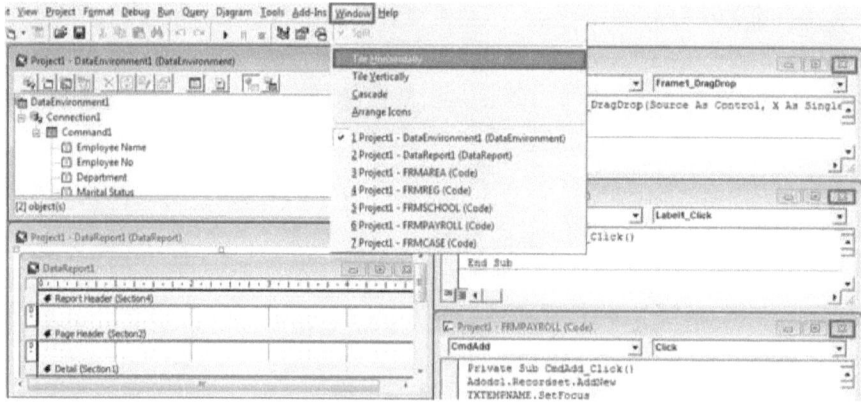

120

Drag Command1 on DataEnvironment and drop on DataReport1's Deatail (Section 1)

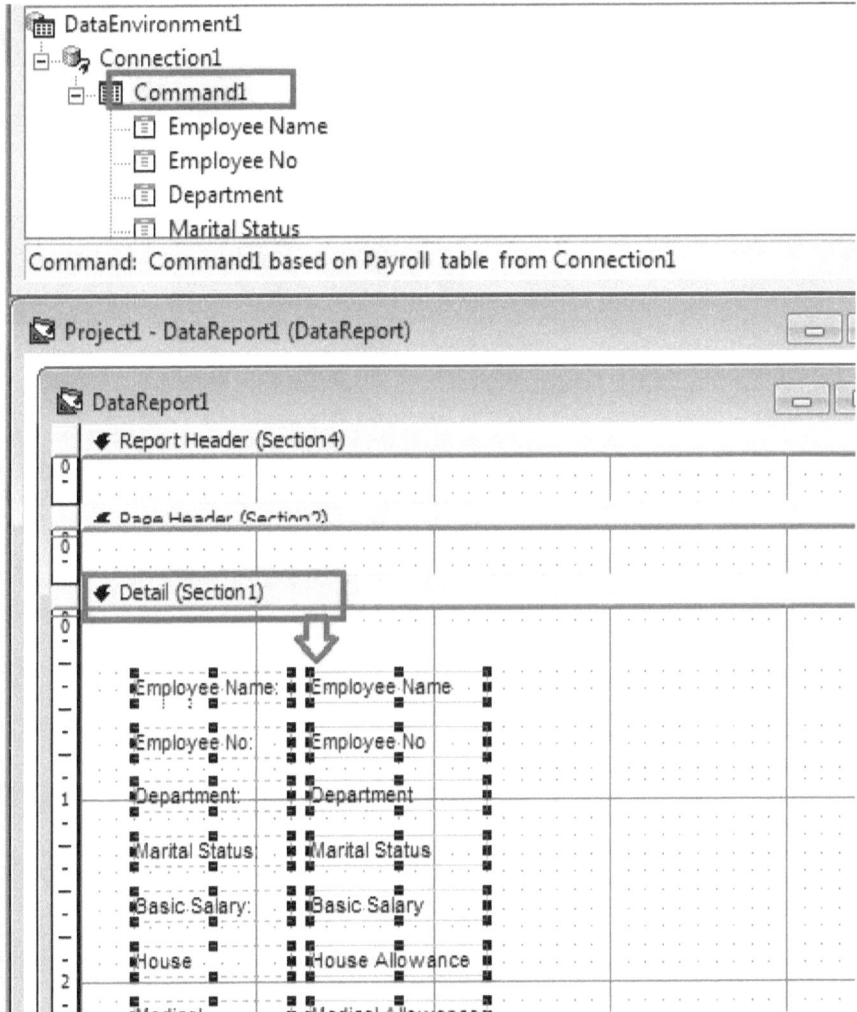

Command: Command1 based on Payroll table from Connection1

Arrange the fields and records in a logical manner, that is fields on page header (Section 2) and records on Detail (Section1). Alternatively, if they fail to fit, on Detail (Section 1), arrange fields on the left and records on right.

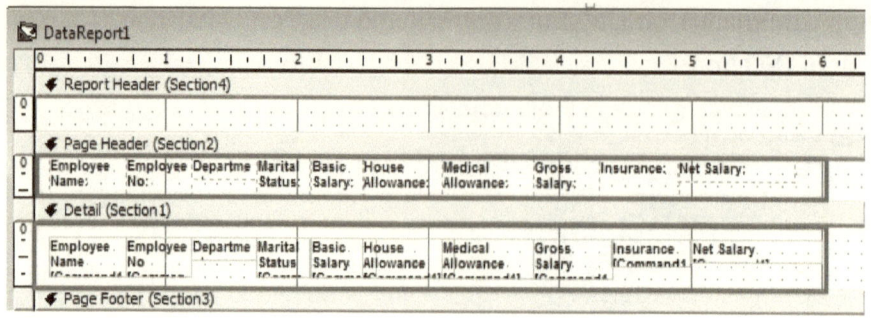

Click on DataReport1 and change the report properties as follows

DataMember - **Command1**

DataSource - **DataEnvironment**

Save your report

To run the report we need to make it as the start up object. Do this choosing Project Menu then Project1 Properties.

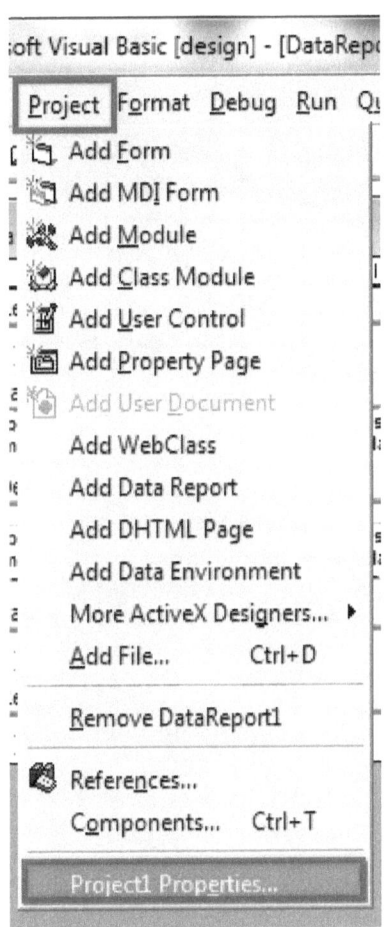

Choose DataReport1 as the Startup object.

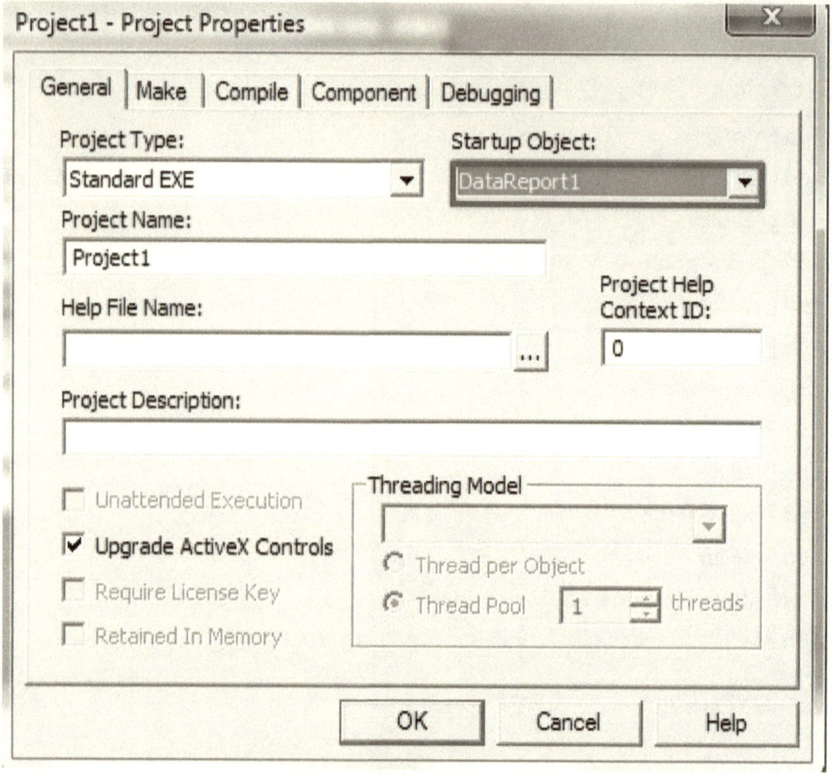

Project1 - Project Properties   X

General | Make | Compile | Component | Debugging |

Project Type: Startup Object:

Standard EXE   ▼   DataReport1   ▼

Project Name:

Project1

Help File Name: Project Help
                                           Context ID:

.... [...]   0

Project Description:

☐ Unattended Execution   ┌─Threading Model──────────
☑ **Upgrade ActiveX Controls**
                                          ▼
☐ Require License Key   ○ Thread per Object
☐ Retained In Memory   ● Thread Pool 1 ⬍ threads

          OK   Cancel   Help

Run the project and here is the report

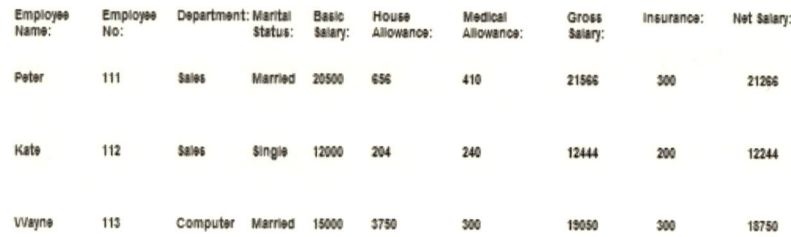

Employee Name:	Employee No:	Department:	Marital Status:	Basic Salary:	House Allowance:	Medical Allowance:	Gross Salary:	Insurance:	Net Salary:
Peter	111	Sales	Married	20500	656	410	21566	300	21266
Kate	112	Sales	Single	12000	204	240	12444	200	12244
Wayne	113	Computer	Married	15000	3750	300	19050	300	18750

We have a printable copy of the payroll form.

Exercise

a) Insert a header "**Payroll**" and a footer "**Net Salary**"

124

b) Insert a line between the fields and the records
c) Create a report on the water application we discussed on the previous chapter

Enhancing the Interface

When you have several forms in a VB project, only one form (startup object) runs. Here, we want to create a parent form (**MDI**) and then set each of the other forms as its children.

Before we create MDI form, we start with **Splash screen** followed by Form **Login**.

Login form is meant to verify the user before granting access to use the project.

Splash Form

A splash screen is a screen that is shown as a program is loading. Splash screen is used for the following reasons:

a) To show a program is loading

b) To show introductory information to the user such as product name and version

c) Copyright information

d) Warning

You can use splash-screen in your project to make it more eye-catching. The splash should be set to appear before the **Login** and **MDI** forms.

To create a Splash Form

Right click Project Explorer, Choose Add then Form

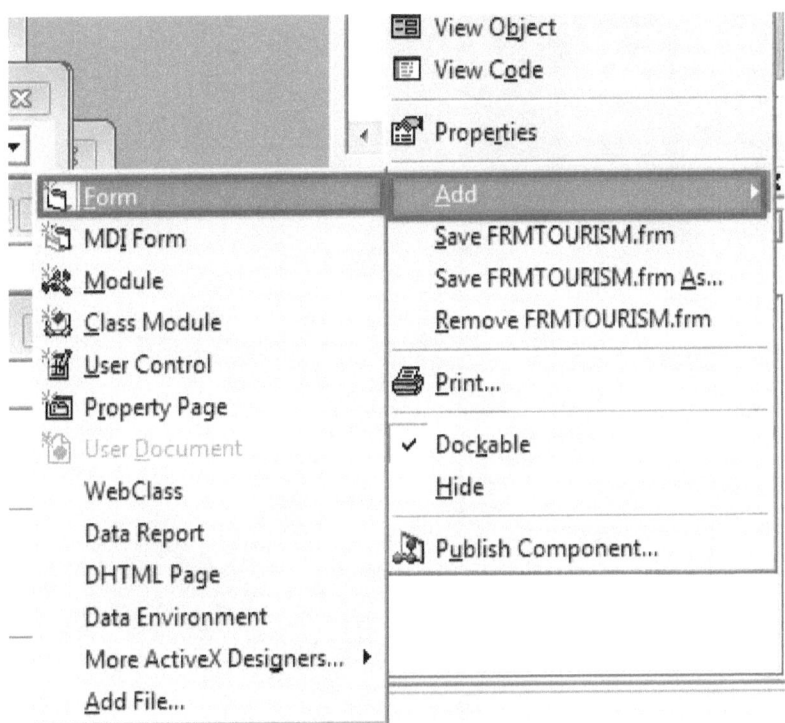

Alternatively, on the Project menu, click **Add Form**.

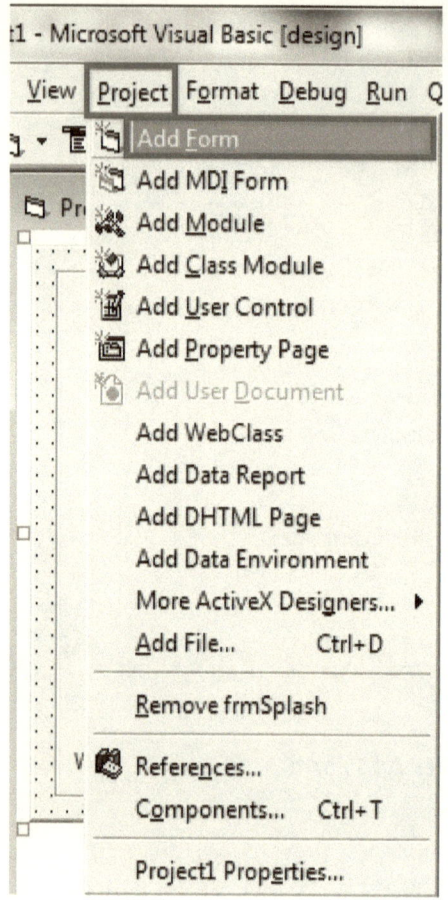

This will bring **Add Form** window and select **Splash Screen**.

128

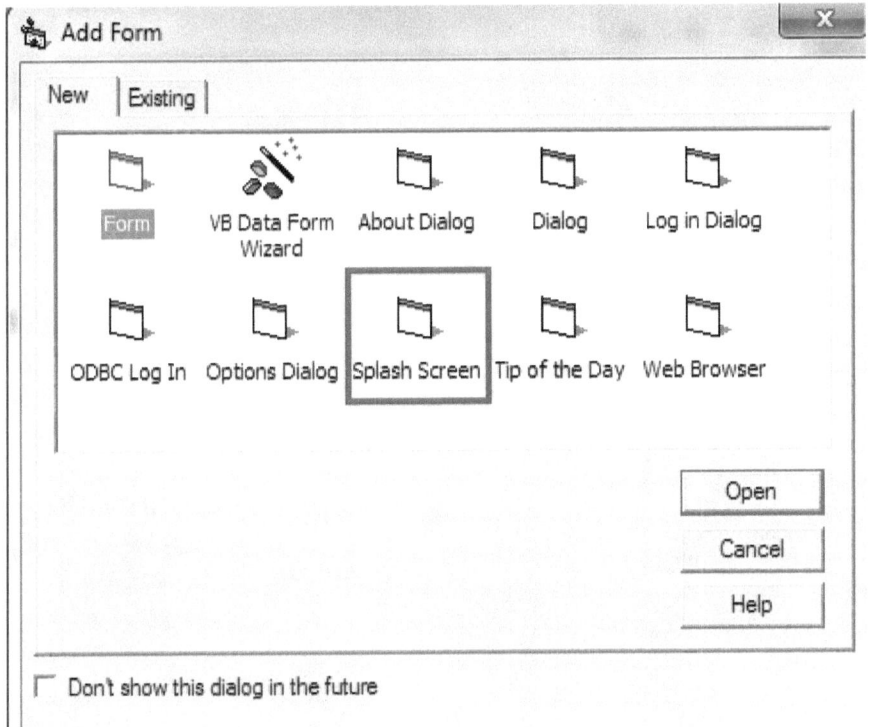

Click Open. This will bring a frmSplash

Login Form

Login form is meant to verify the user before granting access to use the project.

To create a Login Form

Right click Project Explorer, Choose Add then Form

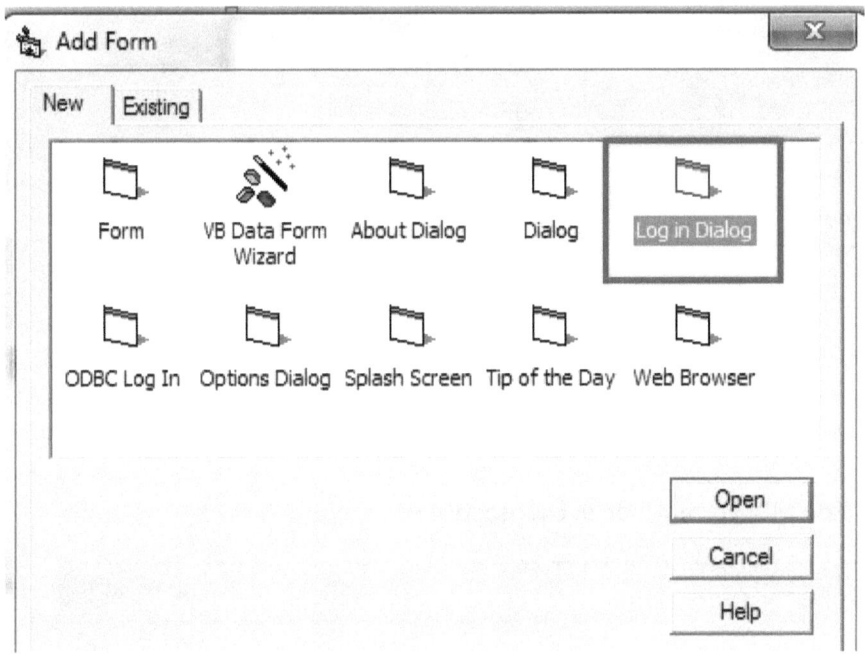

Click Open. This brings frmLogin

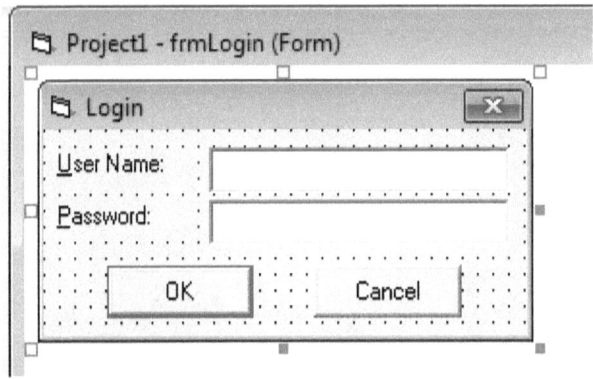

To create a MDI Form

Right click Project Explorer, Choose Add then MDI Form

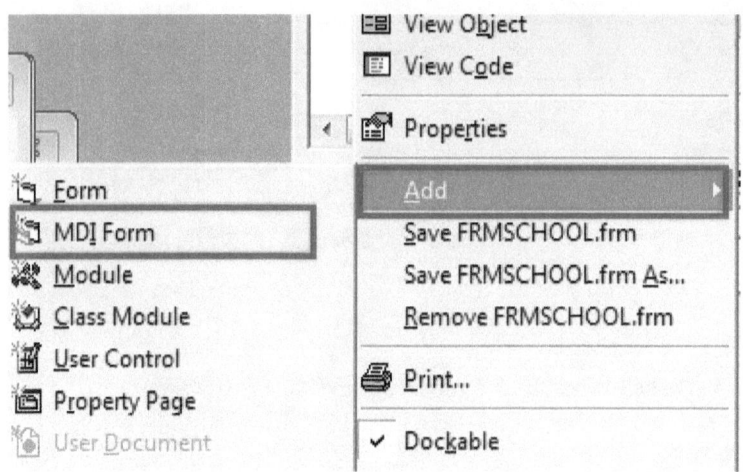

On Add MDI Form window, choose MDI Form

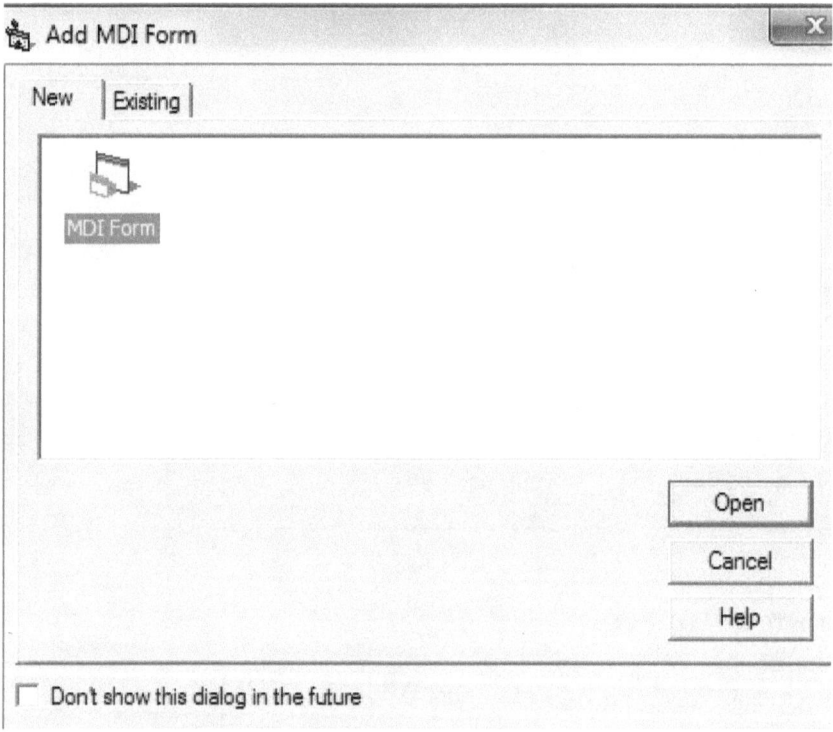

Click Open. This brings MDI Form

Coding Splash Form

Double click frmSplash from the project explorer

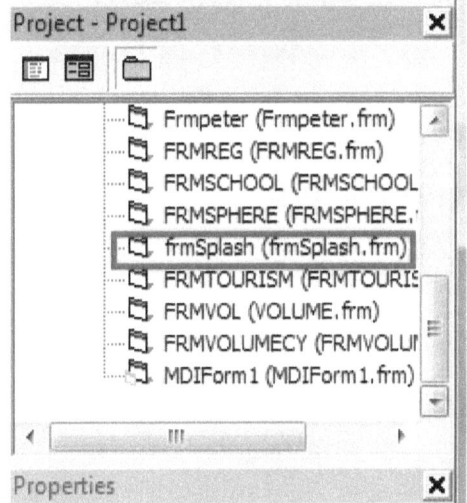

This brings us back to the form we added.

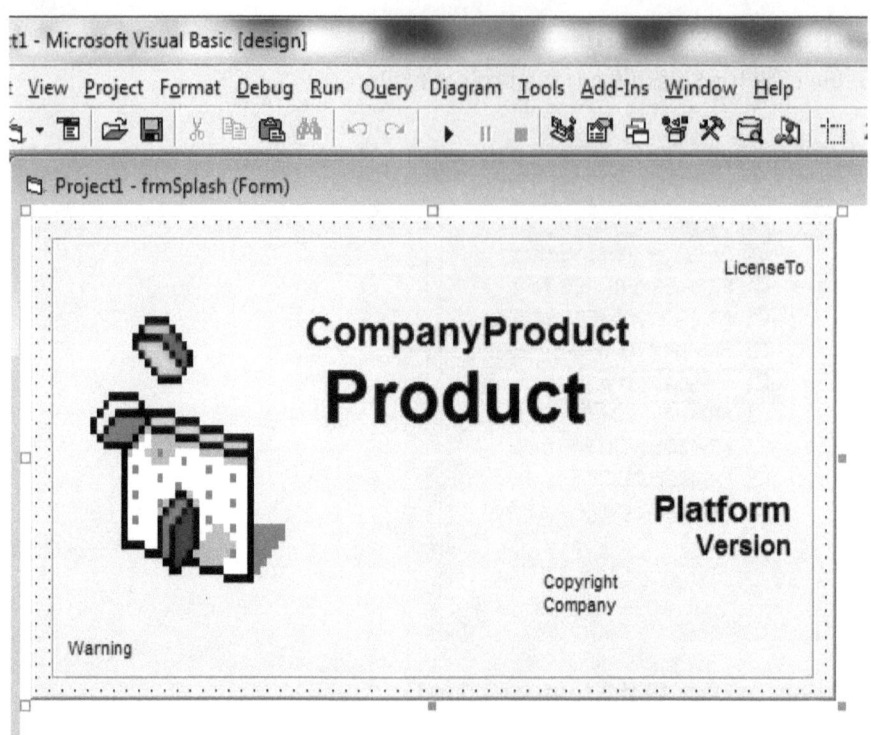

Edit the existing information. Here is an example:

Remember the form you want to load after the splash screen is frmLogin. We can use three ways to load frmLogin:

a. Command Button

b. Timer

c. Progress bar

Using Command Button to load Form Login

Add two commands, name the Enter and Exit

135

Double click Cmdenter to code. Here we type the next form that is, frmLogin.

```
Private Sub CmdEnter_Click()
Frmlogin.Show

End Sub
```

Double click command Exit to code.

```
Private Sub CmdEnter_Click()
End

End Sub
```

NB Delete everything under *Private Sub Form_Load()*

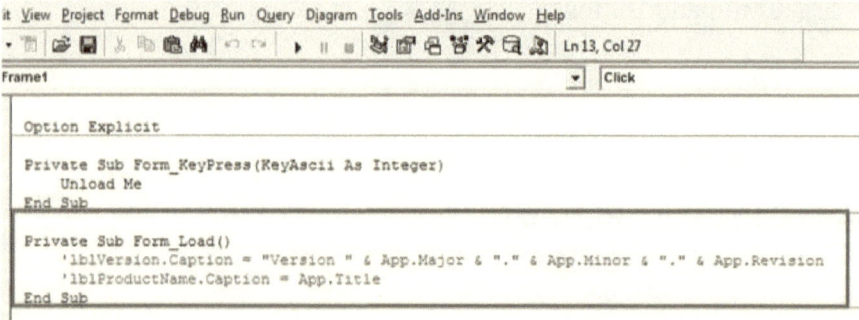

We are done! Set frmSplash as the startup object, run the project, click command Enter. This will load frmLogin.

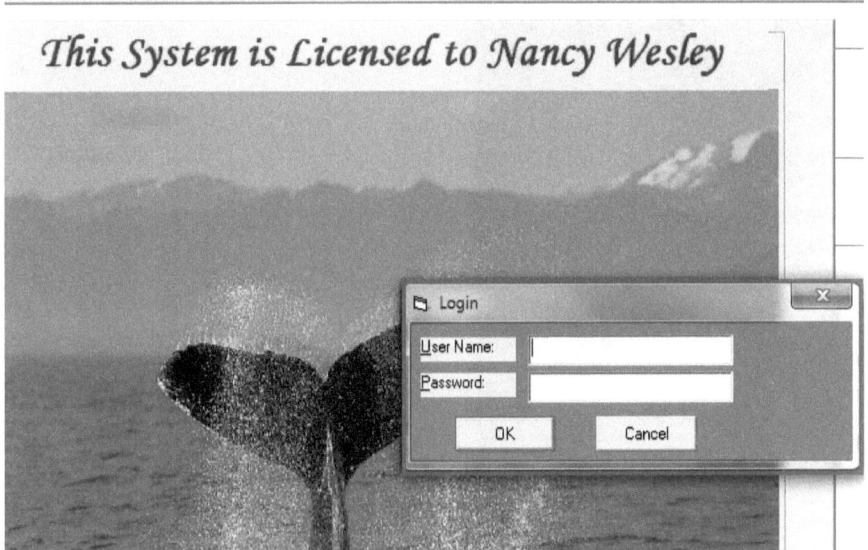

This System is Licensed to Nancy Wesley

Using Timer Control to load Form Login

Insert a timer control on the splash screen form. Set the interval property, for example 1 second, set the Timer's Interval property to 1000, for 3 seconds, set the Timer's Interval property to 3000,

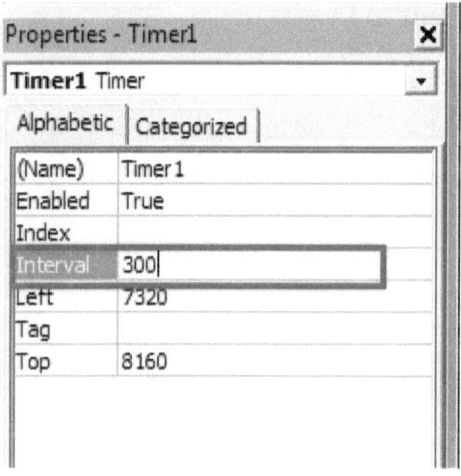

Double click the timer and write the following code in the Timer's Timer Event. We want to load frmLogin after the splash screen.

```
Private Sub Timer1_Timer()
Timer1.Enabled = False
frmLogin.Show
Unload Me
End Sub
```

After we run the project, the splash screen stays for 3 seconds and then form Login is shown after the splash form is unloaded.

Using Progress barto load Form Login

A progress bar shows the user the status of the processing. To use it:

a. From the Menu bar click **Project** and choose **Components**

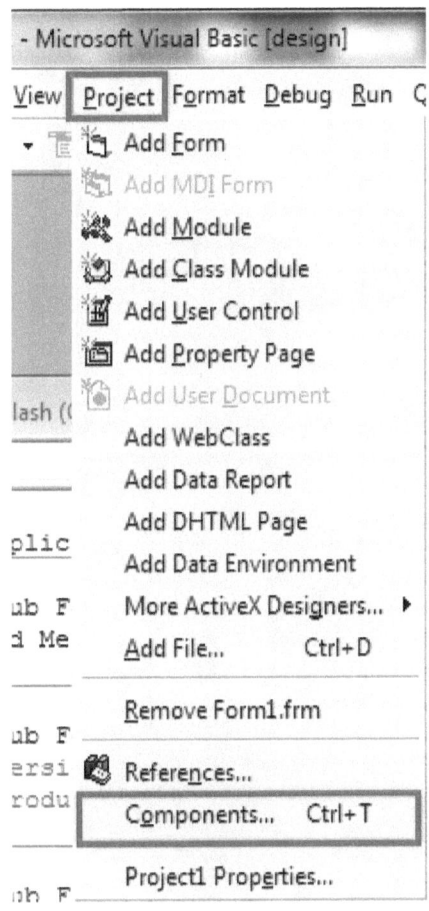

b. On components window check **Microsoft Windows Common Controls 6.0 (SP6)**

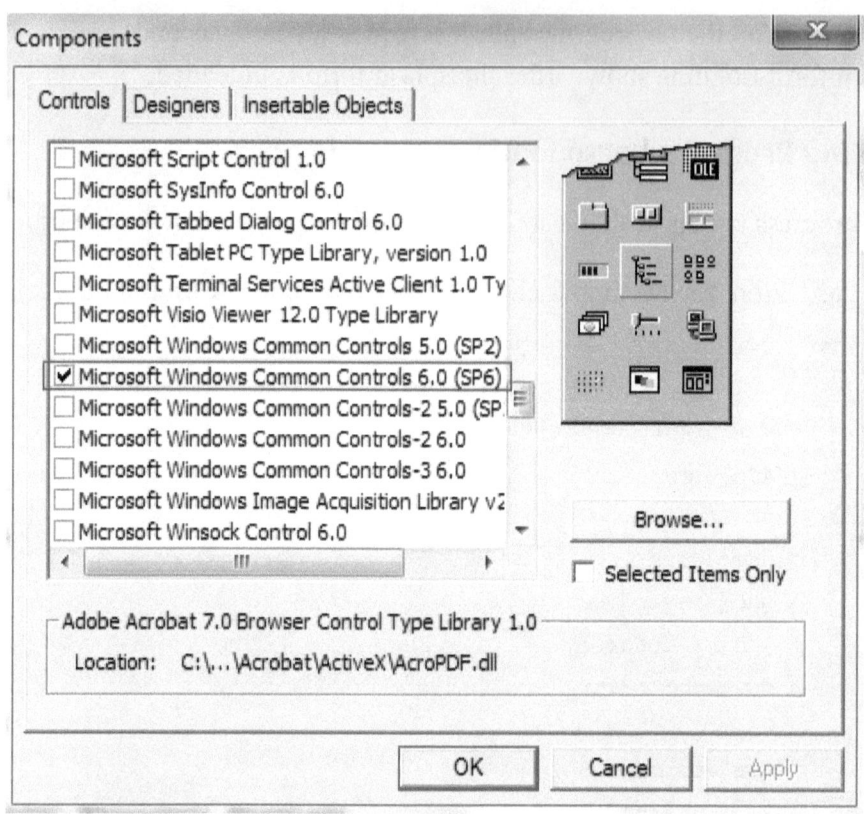

c. Click **Apply** and then **Ok and** the control will appear on the tool box

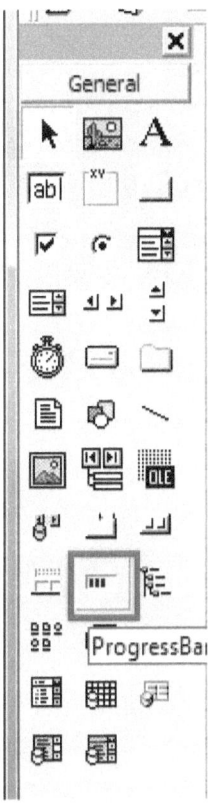

d. Drag a progress bar control onto the form

e. Insert timer control and set interval, for example 300 for three seconds

f. Double click timer control to code:

```
Private Sub Timer1_Timer()
Me.ProgressBar1.Value = Me.ProgressBar1.Value + 1
If Me.ProgressBar1.Value = 100 Then
Unload Me
```

```
frmLogin.Show
Else
End If
```

End Sub

Note the statement `frmLogin.Show` which loads the next form, which is frmLogin.

We have looked at three ways to load form Login from form Splash.

Coding Login Form

Double click **frmLogin** on the project explorer

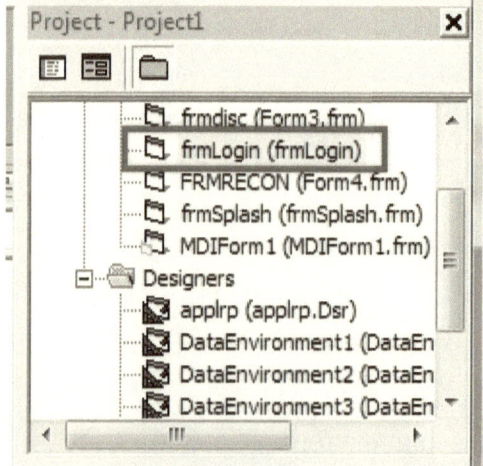

Double click command **Ok** to code

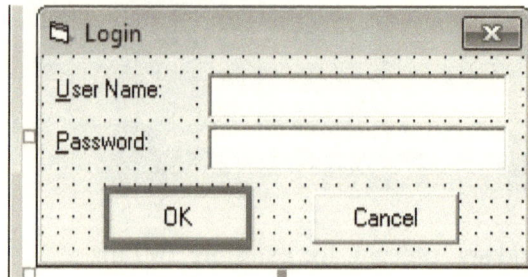

Private Sub cmdOK_Click()
```
'check for correct password
If txtUserName.Text = "nancy" And txtPassword.Text
= "wesley" Then
```
MDIForm1.Show
```
Me.Hide
Unload Me
```

```
Else
MsgBox "Invalid Password, try again!", , "Login"
txtUserName.Text = ""
txtPassword.Text = ""
txtUserName.SetFocus
```

End Sub

This commands checks for correct username and password and loads
MDIform if both are true. It brings the message "Invalid Password,
try again!" if any of them is incorrect.
Double click command Cancel to code:
Private Sub cmdCancel_Click()
```
End
```

End Sub

Coding MDIForm
One can create a menu system to enable call any form at will.
On Tools menu click Menu Editor

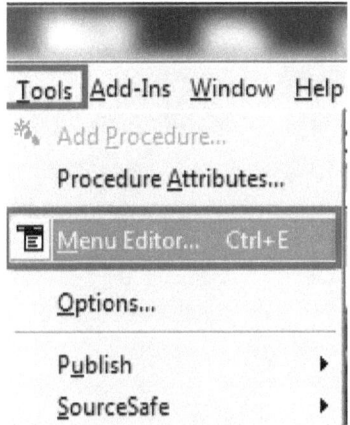

Alternatively, one can just right click anywhere on the MDiForm
and choose Menu Editor. This will load Menu Editor window.

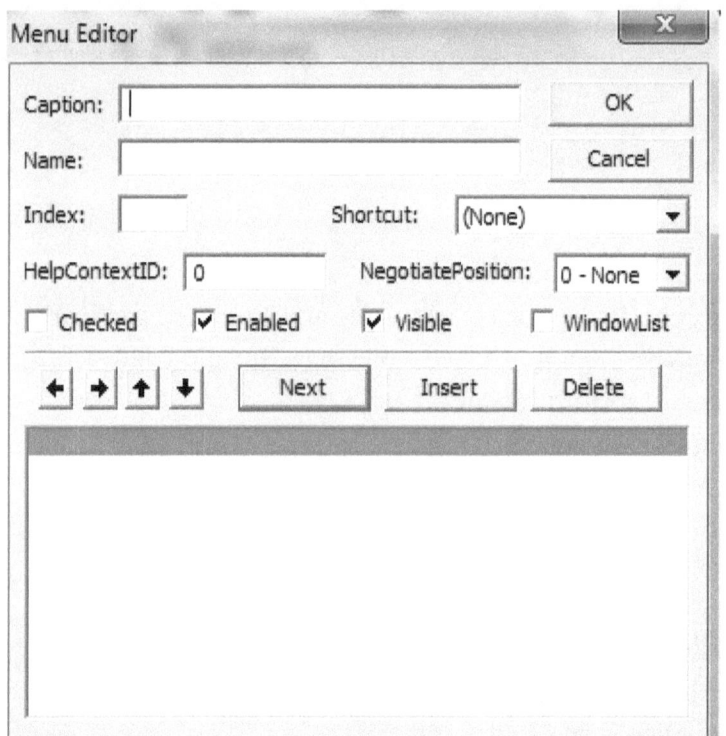

In the **Caption** textbox, type the menu caption (the name that will appear on the menu bar). In the **Name** textbox, type the menu name. The name starts with "Mnu" acronym.

Example

Caption – *File*

Name – *MnuFile*

Click **Next**

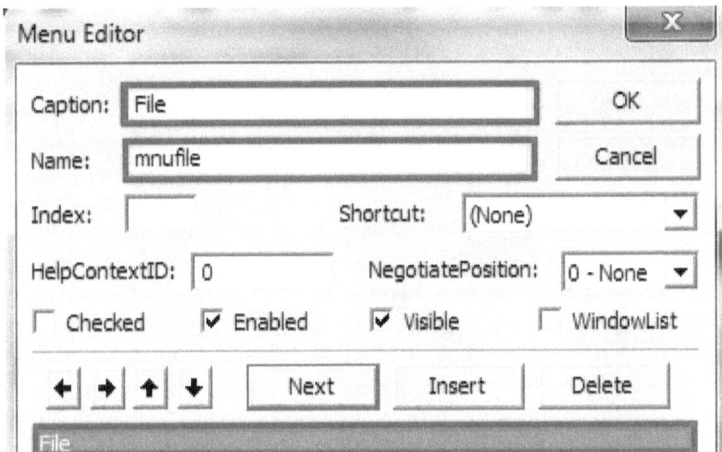

Click **Next**

Here, let's include another menu.

Caption – *Exit*

Name – *MnuExit*

This menu should come under menu File. Here we click the forward allow once.

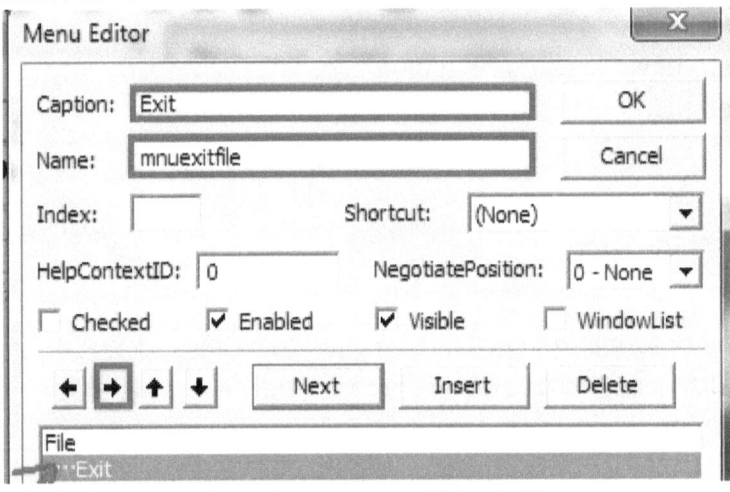

Click **Ok** to see how the menus will look like.

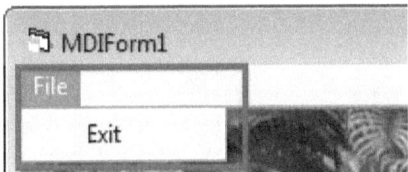

Click **Next** to create another menu.

Caption – *View*

Name – *MnuView*

This menu should not be under menu Exit so we click the allow facing left.

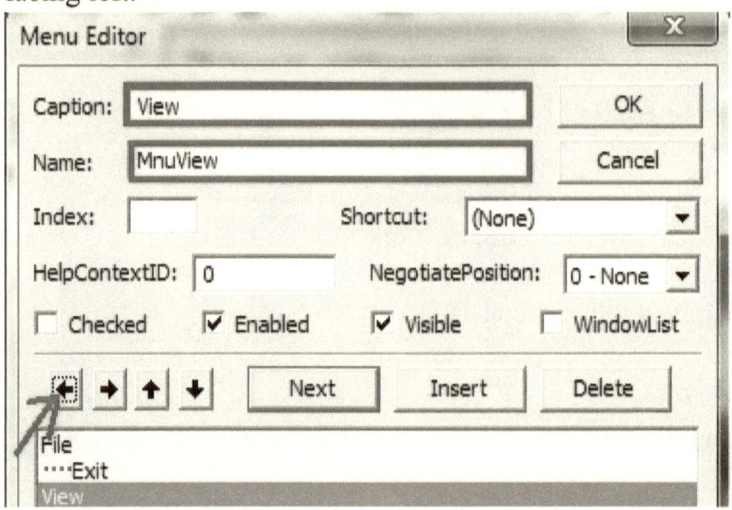

Click **Ok** to see how the menus will look like. Menu view will not be under menu file.

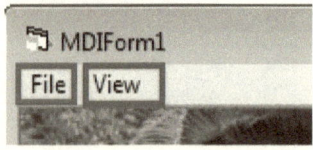

I have three more forms so I need three menus under menu View. I click **Next.i also** need to move one point to the right so I use the arrow to the right.

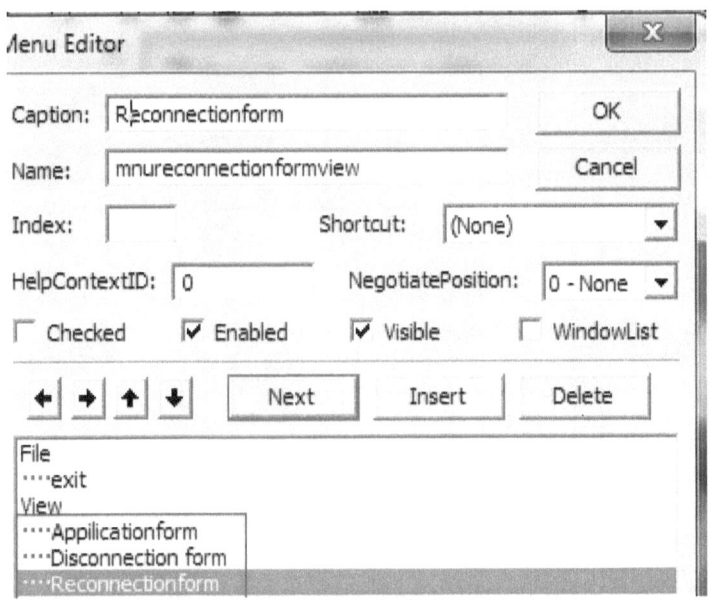

Click **Ok** to see how the menus will look like. Three menus will be under menu View.

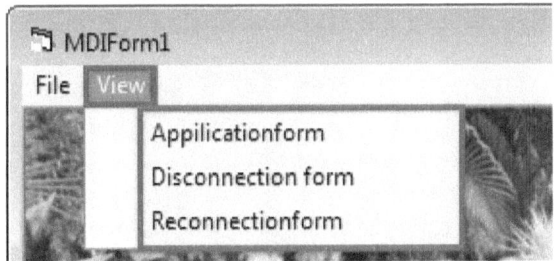

Finally we include the three reports to the Menu. First we create menu Report and three menus to come under it. When creating menu report, we click the arrow to left once since we want menu report to be on the top. For the three menus click the arrow to the right once since we want them to come under menu report.

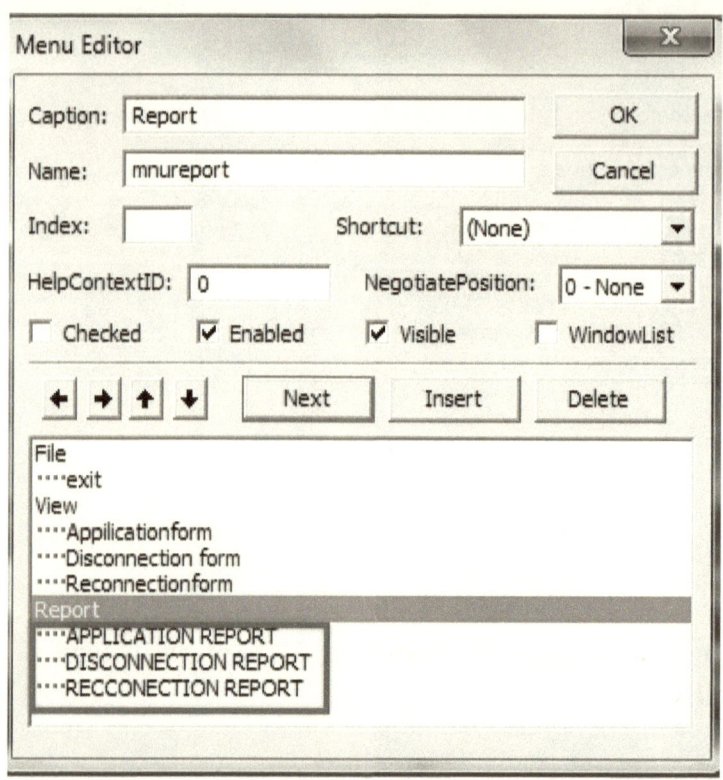

Click **Ok** to see how the menus will look like.

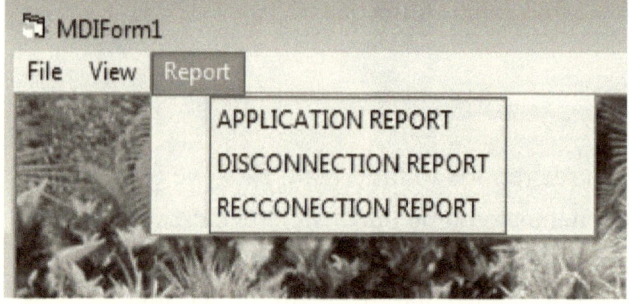

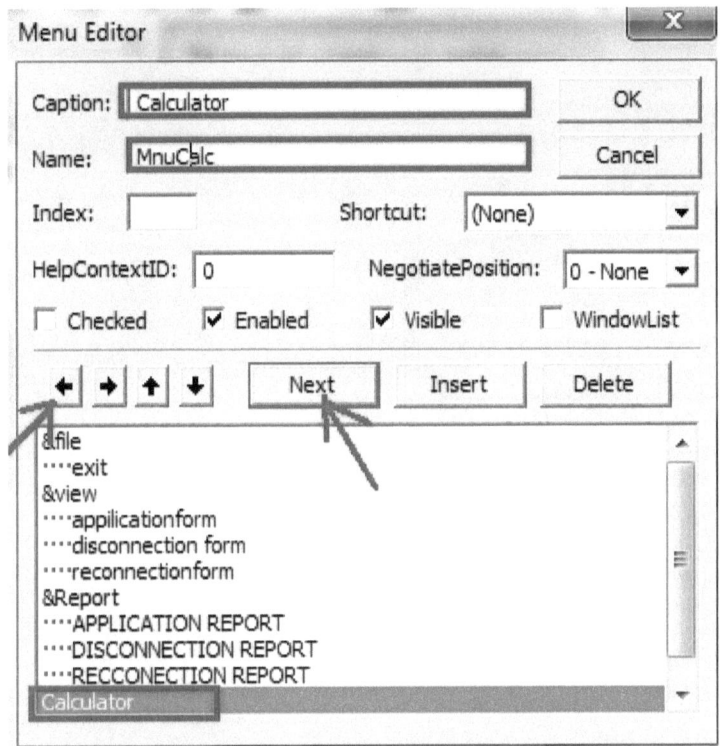

Finally, we assign the menus to the forms and the reports. That is, we click each menu and we type the name of the form or the report to open.

We start checking the names of the forms and the reports from the project explorer.

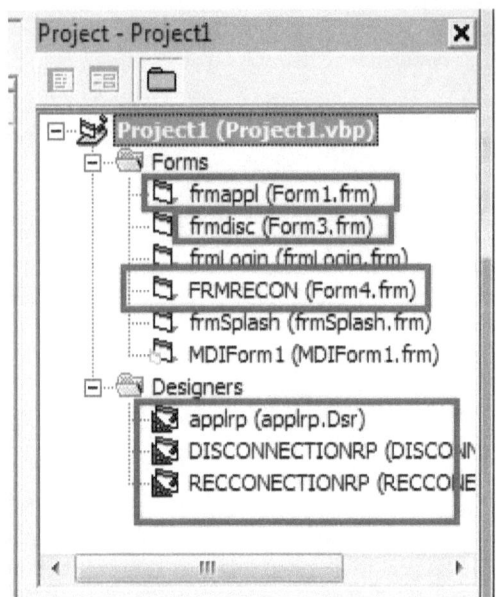

We go back to the MDIForm, we click each of the menus and we type the name of the forms and the reports.

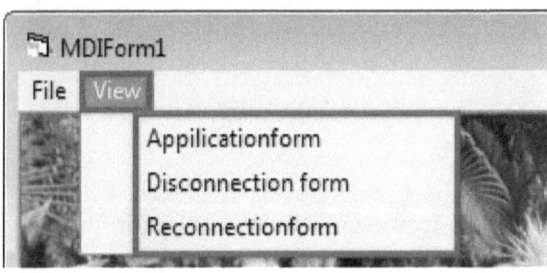

```
Private Sub mnuappilicationformreport_Click()
applrp.Show

End Sub

Private Sub mnuapplicationformview_Click()
frmappl.Show

End Sub

Private Sub mnudisconnectionformreport_Click()
DISCONNECTIONRP.Show

End Sub

Private Sub mnudisconnectionformview_Click()
frmdisc.Show

End Sub

Private Sub mnuexitfile_Click()
Unload Me

End Sub
Private Sub mnureconnectionformreport_Click()
RECCONECTIONRP.Show

End Sub
Private Sub mnureconnectionformview_Click()
FRMRECON.Show

End Sub
```

Suppose we want a windows calculator on a menu. Go back to the Menu Editor, select the last menu, and click next, type Name and Caption. Click the arrow to the left because we don't want the menu to be under menu reconnection report.

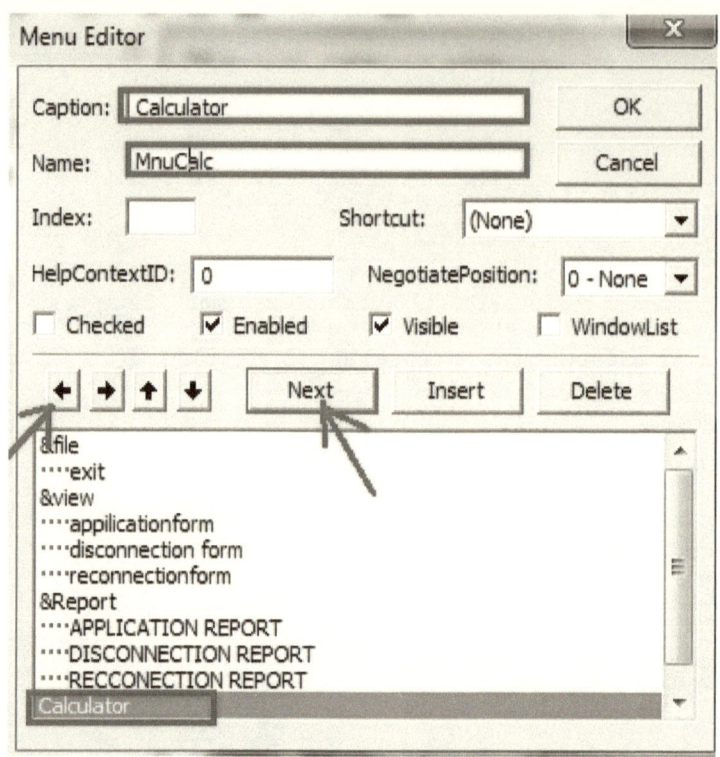

Click OK. Look at the result.

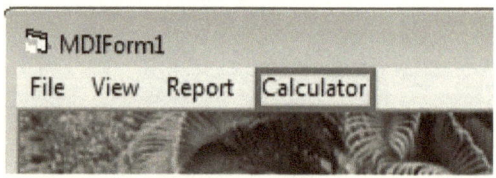

Click the new menu calculator to code.

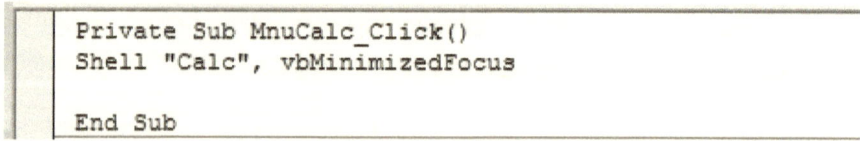

```
Private Sub MnuCalc_Click()
Shell "Calc", vbMinimizedFocus

End Sub
```

Click the menu calculator.

Change the startup object to read FrmSplash. Run the project. Here we find that the project starts with splash, the login and finally MDIForm. If you click any menu the form will run normally without having to change the start up object each time we use any form. Save the project and run it.

Exercise

Enhance the interface for all the forms we created previously by making sure they run under MDIForm and after forms splash and login.

ToolBar Control in Visual Basic 6 (VB6)

Toolbars are found in nearly every application. Toolbars present functionality to a user through a simple accessible, graphical interface, so the user does not need to use a menu. Most widespread features found through buttons on a toolbar.

Creating a Toolbar

Choose a form which will be the main one. Click on **Project** menu and choose **Components**. On components window choose Microsoft Windows Common Controls 5.0 (SP2). Click **Apply** and then **Ok**.

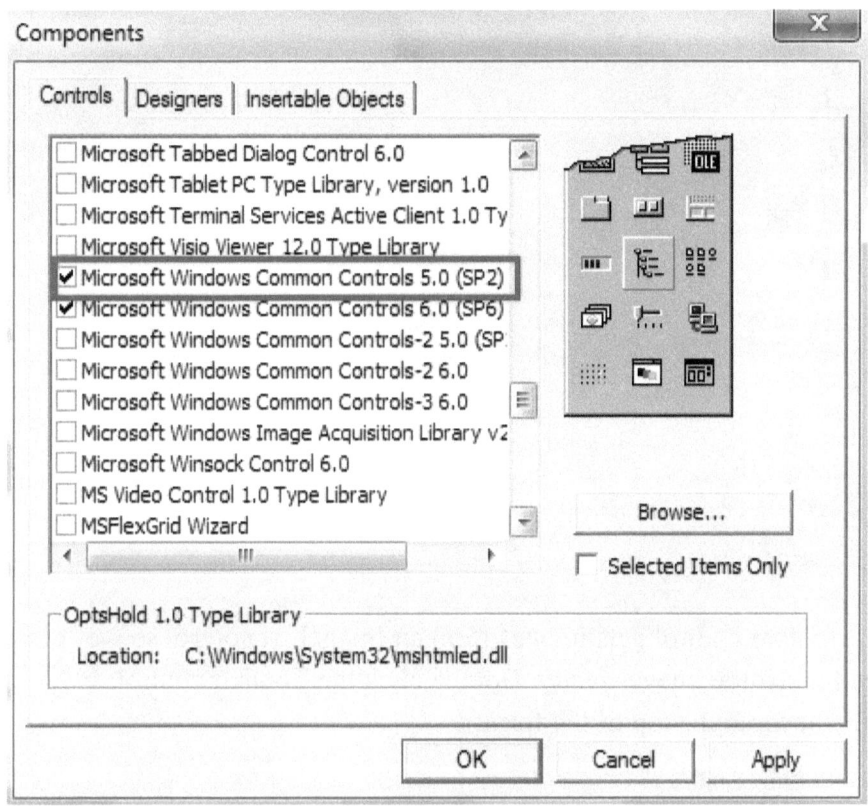

The **Toolbar** and the **ImageList** controls appear on the Toolbox.

The toolbar control gets images from an ImageList control so we need to get the images ready. Double click the Toolbar control. It will appear at the top of the form.

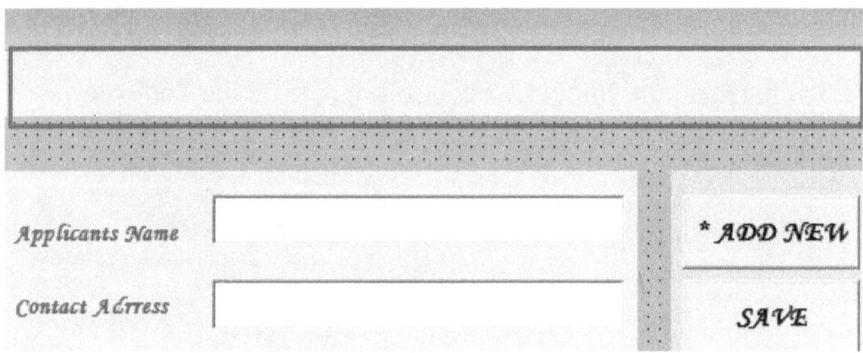

Double click the Toolbar control. It will appear the form.

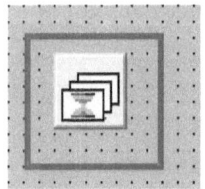

Add Pictures to a ImageList Control

Right click ImageList control. Choose **Properties**.

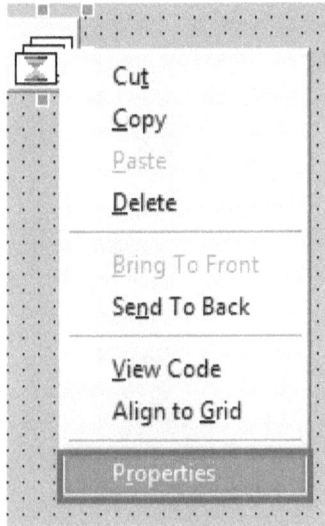

On **Property Pages**, choose **Images** tab and then **Insert Picture** button.

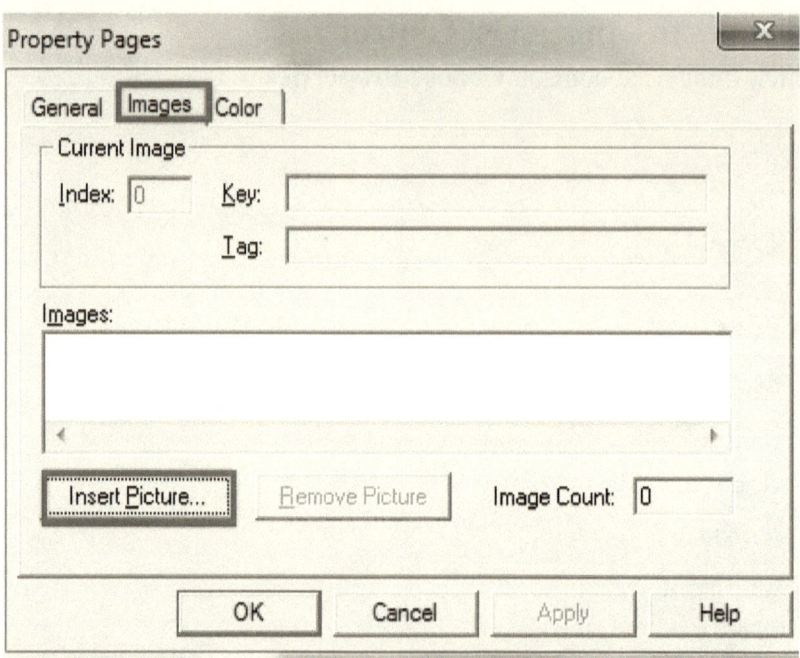

Select the picture you want to appear on the toolbar because the toolbar control gets images from this imagelist control.

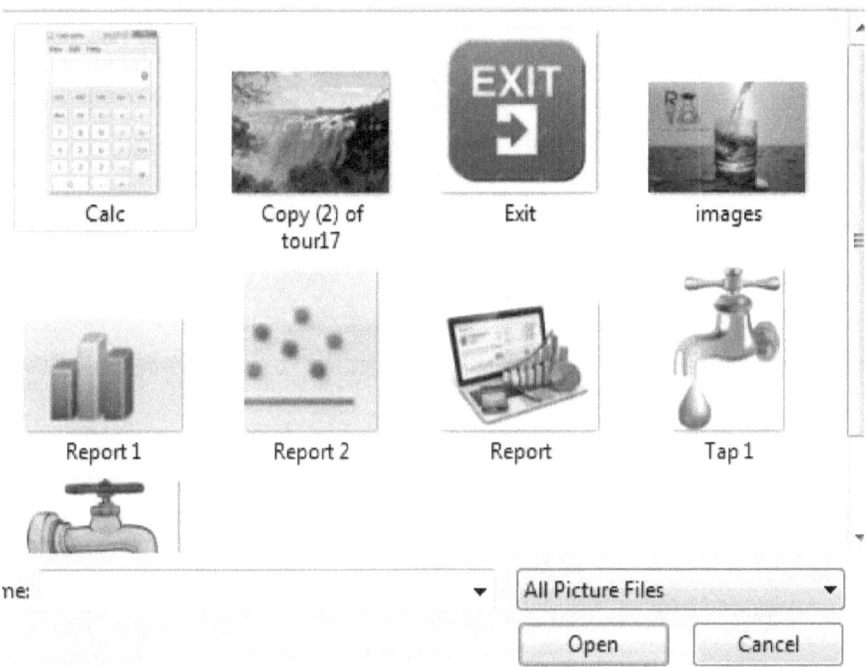

Click Open to insert them.

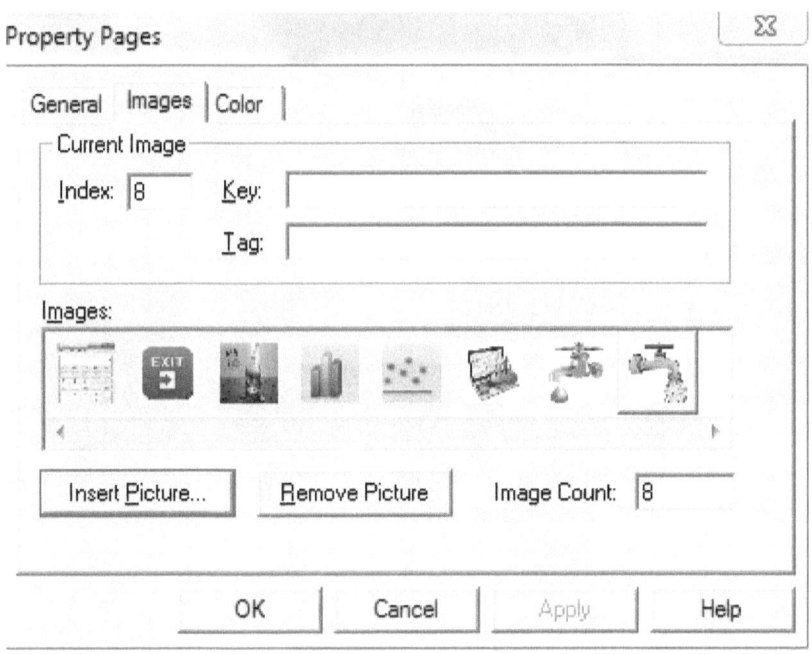

159

Click **Ok**.

The ImageList control has the pictures ready. Lets continue to the ToolBar control.

Right click the ToolBar control and choose properties.

Choose **General** Tab. Choose our ImageList control under the ImageList pull down. Here I choose ImageList1. This is the most important step since it links the toolbar control to the ImageList control.

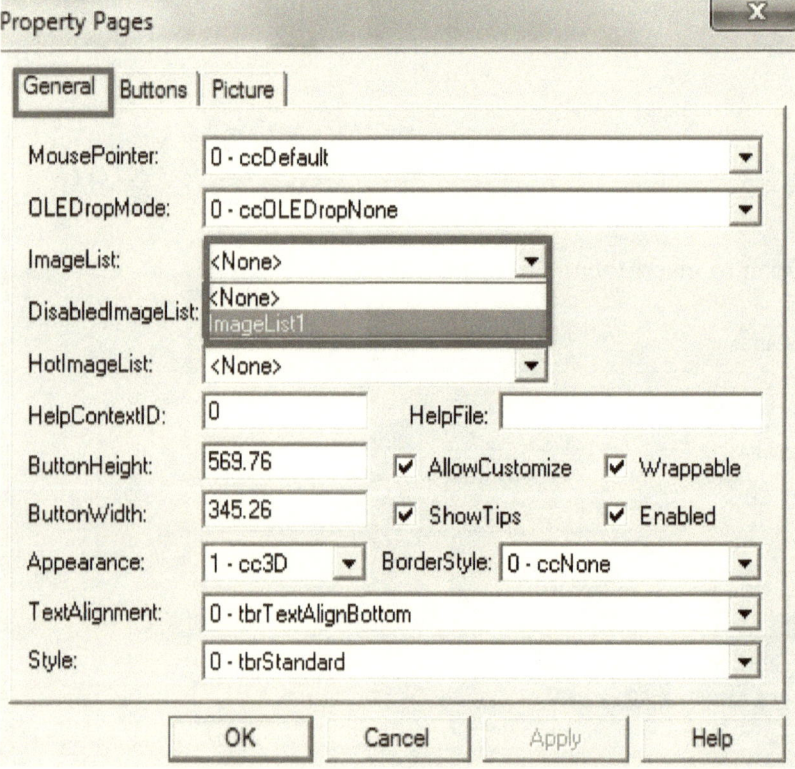

Select the button tab. Here we insert the buttons.

Click **Insert Button**, under the **Image** textbox type the image number. You choose the number depending on the image you prefer to appear on the button.

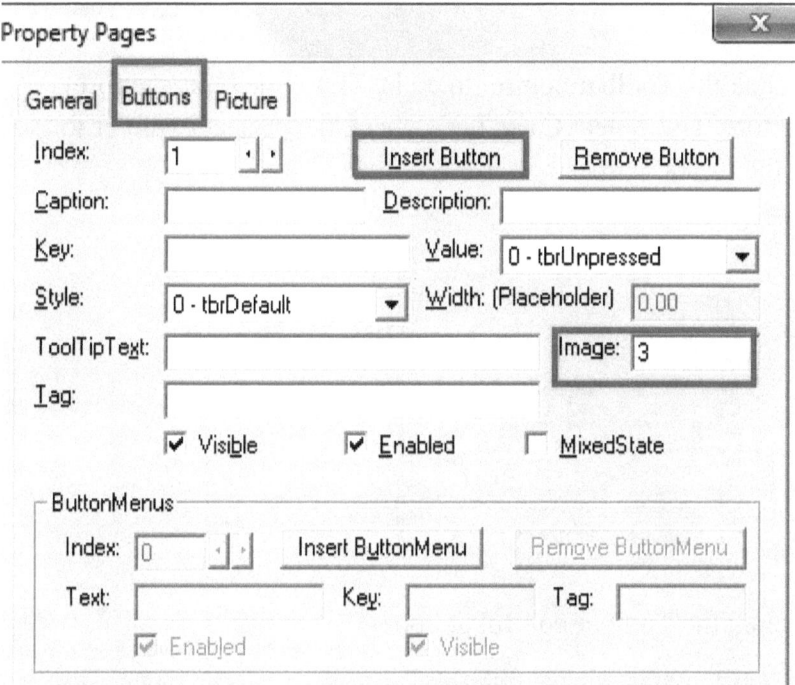

Click Apply and you see the image on the button you inserted. Click insert Button again and choose image to create the second button and to insert the image. You repeat the procedure until you create all your buttons and images displayed. Here I have four forms, Exit and calculator so I have six buttons.

Click Ok to close after you finish.

Double click the Toolbar control to code. This code links the forms to the buttons. Use Select Case. Let's check the project explorer to confirm the forms' names.

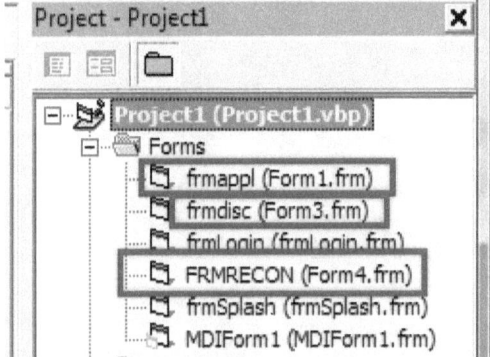

Double click the Toolbar control to code.

```
Private Sub Toolbar1_ButtonClick(ByVal Button As MSComctlLib.Button)
Select Case Button.Index
Case Is = 1
Call frmappl.Show
Case Is = 2
Call frmdisc.Show
Case Is = 3
Call FRMRECON.Show
Case Is = 4
Shell "Calc", vbMaximizedFocus
Case Is = 5
End
End Select

End Sub
```

Exercise

Create a toolbar for the previous projects and use a tool tip text on all the buttons

Procedures and Functions

It's when programs are broken into smaller logical components.

Advantages of Procedures
    a.   It is easier to debug a program with procedures
    b.   Procedures act as buildings blocks for other programs with slight modifications

Each time a procedure is called, the statements between Sub and End Sub are executed. This is done using their names.

Creating a Procedure
The code window is opened.

The procedure option is chosen from the **Tools** menu

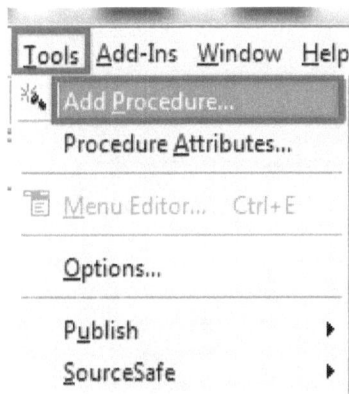

This opens an Add Procedure window

The name of the procedure is typed on the **Name** textbox. Under Type, Sub is selected, under Scope Public is selected.

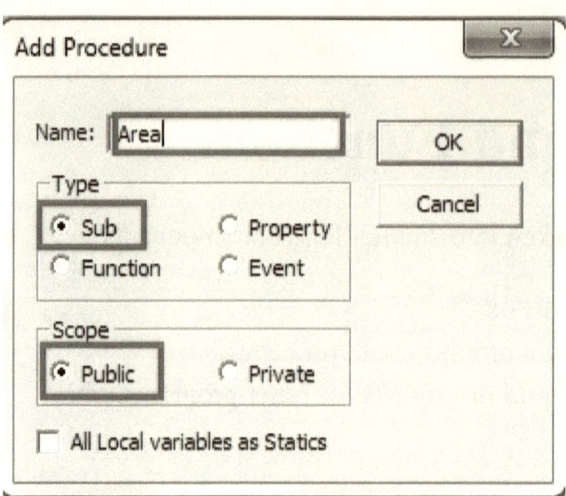

```
Public Sub Area()
Dim L, W As Integer
L = InputBox("Enter Length")
TXTLENGTH.Text = L
W = InputBox("Enter Width")
TXTWIDTH.Text = W
TXTLENGTH.SetFocus
TXTAREA.Text = TXTLENGTH.Text * TXTWIDTH.Text

End Sub
```

```
Public Sub Volume()
Dim r, h As Integer
r = InputBox("Enter the radius")
txtr.Text = r
h = InputBox("Enter the height")
txth.Text = h

p = 3.142
txtv = p * txtr * txtr * txth

End Sub
```

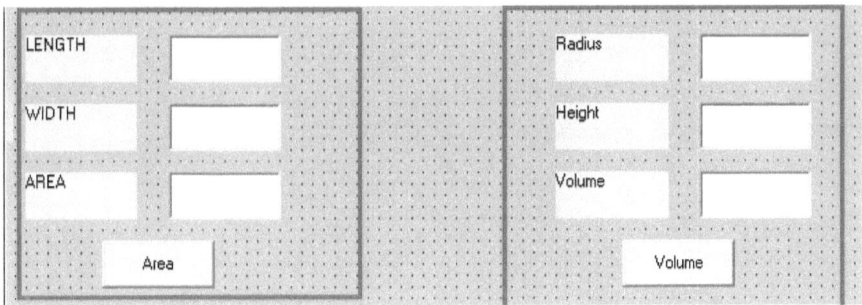

Also one can create a new procedure in the current module by typing sub procedure in the code window.

Here am using a command button to call a procedure anytime.

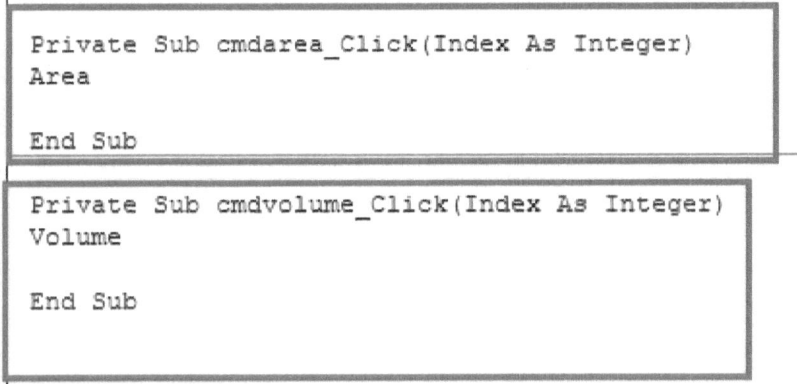

```
Private Sub cmdarea_Click(Index As Integer)
Area

End Sub
```

```
Private Sub cmdvolume_Click(Index As Integer)
Volume

End Sub
```

Run the project. Click any command. This will call a procedure.

Functions

Procedures are used to perform a task while functions are used when we want to get a value. For example let's create a function to convert centimeters to inches.

Create the interface

First Textbox: *Txtcm*

Second Texbox: *TxtInches*

165

Command: *CmdConvert*

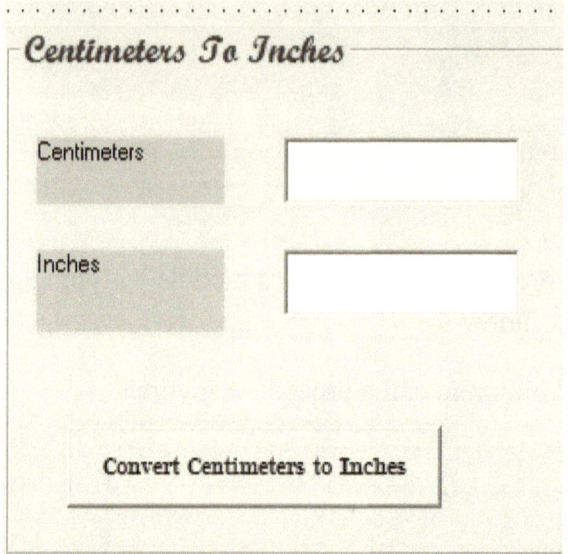

Open the code Window and type Function followed by the function name.

```
Function Cmtoinch(Cmvar As Single) As Single
Cmtoinch = Cmvar / 2.54


End Function
```

Double click command and code

```
Private Sub CmdConvert_Click()
TxtInches.Text = Val(Cmtoinch(Val(Txtcm.Text)))

End Sub
```

Run the program, enter a value to represent the centimeters and click command to convert.

Centimeters To Inches

Centimeters

20

Inches

7.874016

Convert Centimeters to Inches

Animation

We use a simple technique to create an animation by setting the properties Visible to False and Visible to False. True is used to show and False to hide two images alternatively. When you run the program, the animation shows images for example image1, image2 and image3 interchangeably.

Insert the Timer control and set the interval property for example 2000. Let's use four images. Put four image controls on the form and upload four images.

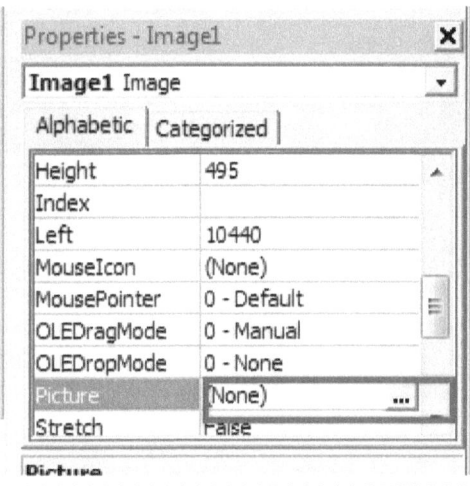

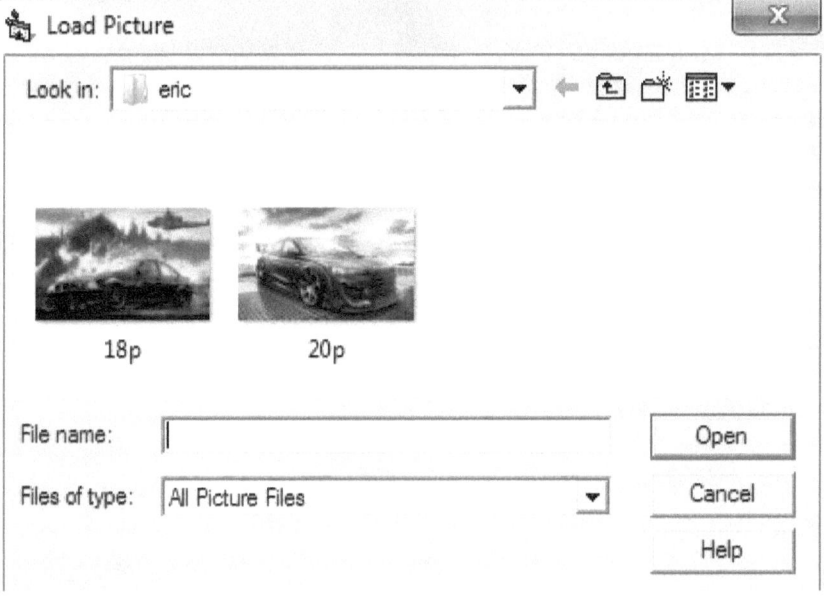

The picture should have the same size. Put the pictures on top of each other.

Double click the Timer control to code:

```
Private Sub Timer1_Timer()
If Image1.Visible = True Then
Image1.Visible = False
Image2.Visible = True
ElseIf Image2.Visible = True Then
Image2.Visible = False
Image3.Visible = True
ElseIf Image3.Visible = True Then
Image3.Visible = False
Image4.Visible = True
ElseIf Image4.Visible = True Then
Image4.Visible = False
Image5.Visible = True
ElseIf Image5.Visible = True Then
Image5.Visible = False
Image1.Visible = True


End Sub
```

Creating an Audio Player

This player works in such a way that it can search for sound files in your drives and play them.

You need to use a **ComboBox**, a **DriveListBox**, a **DirListBox**, a **TextBox** and a **FileListBox** into your form. **Microsoft Multimedia Control(MMControl)** must be inserted into your form. Choose Projects, Components.

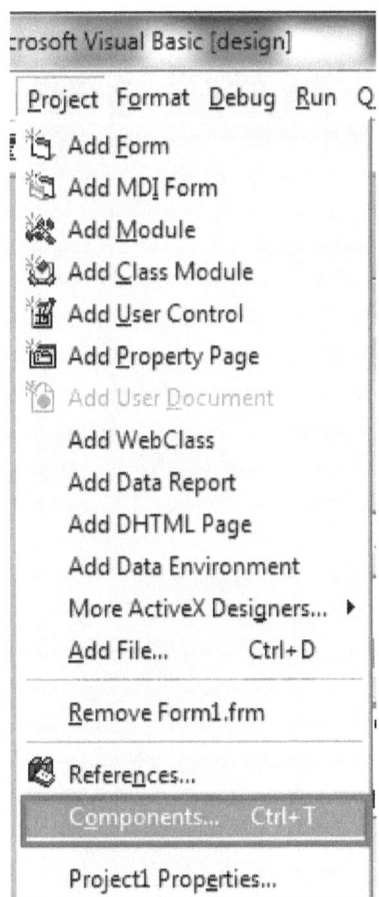

On Components window, select Microsoft Multimedia Control 6.0

Click Apply then Ok.

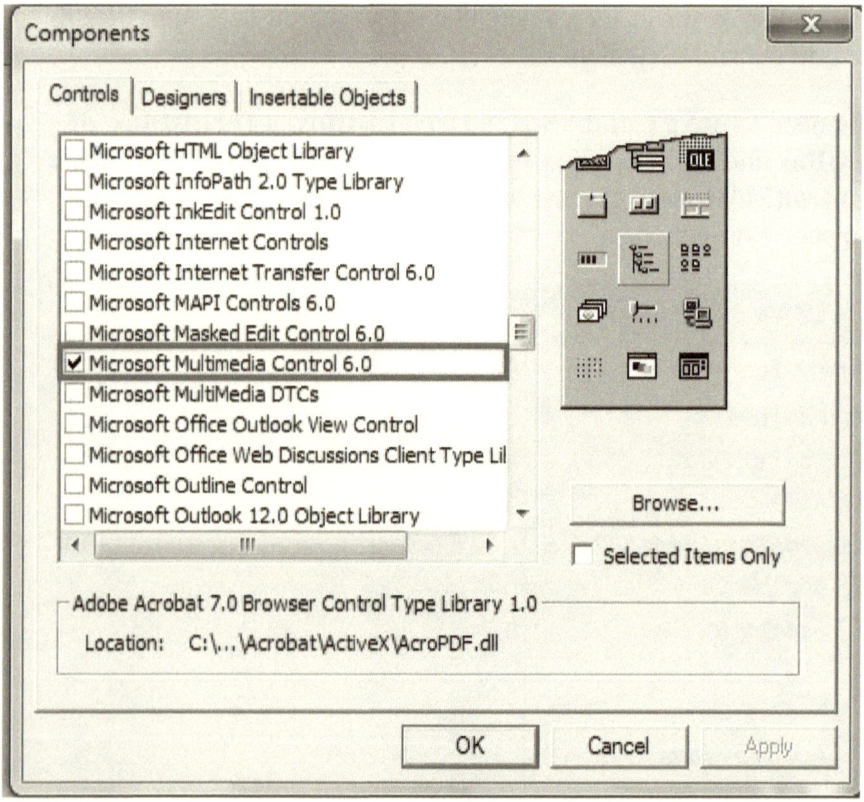

Components

Controls | Designers | Insertable Objects

- [ ] Microsoft HTML Object Library
- [ ] Microsoft InfoPath 2.0 Type Library
- [ ] Microsoft InkEdit Control 1.0
- [ ] Microsoft Internet Controls
- [ ] Microsoft Internet Transfer Control 6.0
- [ ] Microsoft MAPI Controls 6.0
- [ ] Microsoft Masked Edit Control 6.0
- [x] Microsoft Multimedia Control 6.0
- [ ] Microsoft MultiMedia DTCs
- [ ] Microsoft Office Outlook View Control
- [ ] Microsoft Office Web Discussions Client Type Lil
- [ ] Microsoft Outline Control
- [ ] Microsoft Outlook 12.0 Object Library

Browse...

[ ] Selected Items Only

Adobe Acrobat 7.0 Browser Control Type Library 1.0

Location: C:\...\Acrobat\ActiveX\AcroPDF.dll

OK | Cancel | Apply

ComboBox- to display and enable selection of different type of files

DriveListBox- to allow selection selection of different drives available on your PC

172

DirListBox - To display directories

TextBox - To display selected files

FileListBox- To display files that are available

User chooses the type of files to play, selects the drive that might contains audio files, looks into directories and subdirectories for the files. The files should be displayed in the **FileListBox**. User selects the files from the **FileListBox** and clicks the **Play** button.

The **Stop** button stops playing and **Exit** button to closes the application.

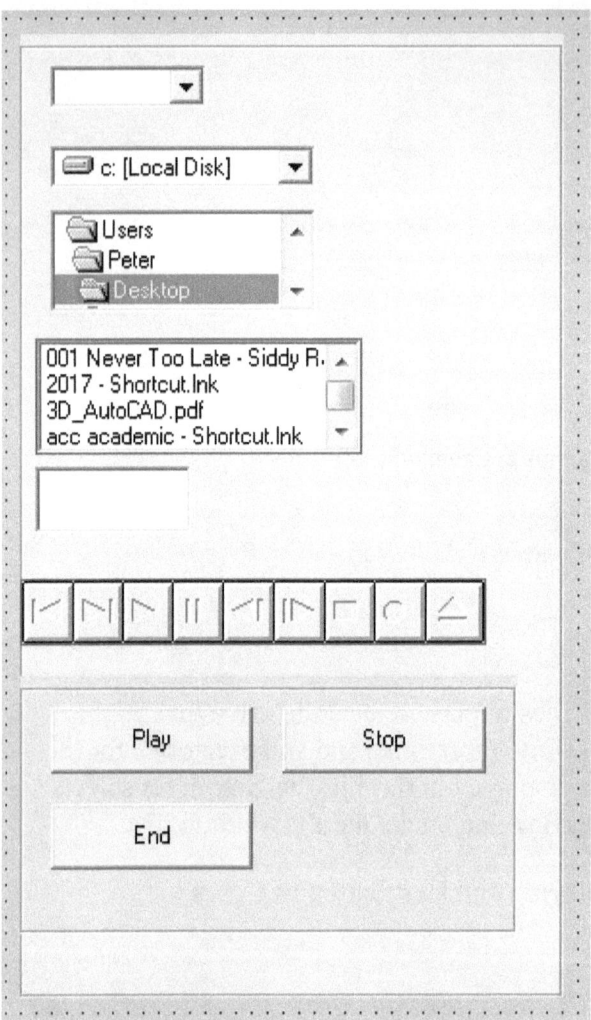

Codes:

Private Sub Combo1_Change()
```
If ListIndex = 0 Then
File1.Pattern = ("*.wav")
ElseIf ListIndex = 1 Then
File1.Pattern = ("*.mid")
Else
Fiel1.Pattern = ("*.*")
End If
```

End Sub

```
Private Sub Cmdplay_Click()
If AudioPlayer.Mode = 524 Then Exit Sub
If AudioPlayer.Mode <> 525 Then
AudioPlayer.Wait = True
AudioPlayer.Command = "Stop"
End If
AudioPlayer.Wait = True
AudioPlayer.Command = "Close"

End Sub

Private Sub Cmdend_Click()
Unload Me

End Sub

Private Sub Cmdstop_Click()
'Command3_Click
If Combo1.ListIndex = 0 Then
AudioPlayer.DeviceType = "WaveAudio"
ElseIf Combo1.ListIndex = 1 Then
AudioPlayer.DeviceType = "Sequencer"
End If
AudioPlayer.FileName = Text1.Text
AudioPlayer.Command = "Open"
AudioPlayer.Command = "Play"
Print ·

End Sub

Private Sub Dir1_Change()
File1.Path = Dir1.Path
If Combo1.ListIndex = 0 Then
File1.Pattern = ("*.wav")
ElseIf Combo1.ListIndex = 1 Then
File1.Pattern = ("*.mid")
Else
File1.Pattern = ("*.*")
End If

End Sub
```

```
Private Sub Drive1_Change()
Dir1.Path = Drive1.Drive


End Sub

Private Sub File1_Click()
If Combo1.ListIndex = 0 Then
File1.Pattern = ("*.wav")
ElseIf Combo1.ListIndex = 1 Then
File1.Pattern = ("*.mid")
Else
File1.Pattern = ("*.*")
End If

If Right(File1.Path, 1) <> "\" Then
filenam = File1.Path + "\" + File1.FileName
Else
filenam = File1.Path + File1.FileName
End If
Text1.Text = filenam

End Sub

Private Sub Form_Load()
Left = (Screen.Width - Width) \ 2
Top = (Screen.Height - Height) \ 2
Combo1.Text = "*.wav"
Combo1.AddItem "*.wav"
Combo1.AddItem "*.mid"
Combo1.AddItem "All files"

End Sub
```

www.ingramcontent.com/pod-product-compliance
Lightning Source LLC
Chambersburg PA
CBHW030634220526
45463CB00004B/1521